INVITE HIS *light*

HEALING TRAUMA
ONE STEP AT A TIME

MOLLY C. MCNAMARA

LIFEWISE BOOKS

INVITE HIS LIGHT
HEALING TRAUMA ONE STEP AT A TIME
BY MOLLY C. MCNAMARA

Scriptures marked KJV are taken from the KING JAMES VERSION (KJV): KING JAMES VERSION, public domain.

Scriptures marked TM are taken from the THE MESSAGE: THE BIBLE IN CONTEMPORARY ENGLISH (TM): Scripture taken from THE MESSAGE: THE BIBLE IN CONTEMPORARY ENGLISH, copyright©1993, 1994, 1995, 1996, 2000, 2001, 2002. Used by permission of NavPress Publishing Group

Scriptures marked NAS are taken from the NEW AMERICAN STANDARD (NAS): Scripture taken from the NEW AMERICAN STANDARD BIBLE®, copyright© 1960, 1962, 1963, 1968, 1971, 1972, 1973, 1975, 1977, 1995 by The Lockman Foundation. Used by permission.

Scriptures marked NIV are taken from the NEW INTERNATIONAL VERSION (NIV): Scripture taken from THE HOLY BIBLE, NEW INTERNATIONAL VERSION ®. Copyright© 1973, 1978, 1984, 2011 by Biblica, Inc.™. Used by permission of Zondervan

Scriptures marked NKJV are taken from the NEW KING JAMES VERSION (NKJV): Scripture taken from the NEW KING JAMES VERSION®. Copyright© 1982 by Thomas Nelson, Inc. Used by permission. All rights reserved.

Published by:

⚓LIFEWISE BOOKS
PO BOX 1072
Pinehurst, TX 77362
LifeWiseBooks.com

To contact the author: hiswholehouse.org

Print - 978-1-958820-14-8

Ebook - 978-1-958820-15-5

DEDICATION

To my spiritual father, Kent Newman,
who helped guide me to the source of truth and light,
Jesus Christ.
I am eternally grateful.

"The more severe the battle, the greater our need for persistence. Persistence is strengthened by our awareness of the greatness of He who stands with us and the companions in battle who stand alongside us. We never stand alone. He never joins us in spiritual battles beyond our ability to fight. Back of 'what happens' is a 'who' that is often causing it. Our eyes must be opened to see the 'who' and 'who' stands with us. As we pray, the Lord dispatches His help and light for our battle."

KENT NEWMAN
1925-2018

SPECIAL THANKS

To my friends and family who encouraged this book and helped listen to me through rehearsals and tears in bringing this guide to life. To Vance and Anna Erickson, Pamela Moore, Robert and Kathie Fetveit, Dana Grindal, and Susan and Dave Brooks for your encouragement to get going and write. To the Whole House team who handled the ministry operations on many days so I could keep the space and time for the work.

Lastly, to my incredibly talented and gifted editors, Charity Bradshaw, Dana Grindal, and Marty McNamara, who lovingly showed me more ways to share a story than can be told on one page. You are my heroes.

CONTENTS

PREFACE

This book is a journey guide for interreflection by the reader and those who can attest to having lost their way and the struggle to find the path back to the light.

Loss has a thousand different faces, and in the tension of today's culture, the demands placed upon us can quickly knock us off balance. Loss can mean all sorts of things, from loss of freedom, financial loss, relationship change, death of a loved one, a life-changing illness, failure of a dream, etc., and each instance is a trauma. Whether or not we embrace the changing landscape determines our ability to walk through a trauma rather than become stuck in it.

You might ask, "How do you know about being stuck in trauma?" I've been given a special place in the world of trauma, partly because of my own traumatic experiences (which were not processed for many years) and as a healthcare provider directing one of the world's largest trauma centers, serving a large metropolitan city in Texas.

On a personal level, the tipping point for my descent into the darkness happened one beautiful day in May of 1998, while the garden was in full spring bloom. It was a perfect day to prepare for the upcoming arrival of my son from Nashville, Tennessee. In less than a month, he was returning home to stay. My days were full of excitement, anticipation, and plans for the long-awaited arrival of my dear Adam Thomas. That day never came.

Instead, I received a call that shattered my heart into a million pieces and flooded my soul with darkness. My son had died by suicide. In an instant, everything changed—my family, community, way of believing, and core life purpose. The following eleven years were spent groping along in the dark, trying to find a way back to the light and life. It has been decades now, and the power of that loss, along with many God-ordained moments, have become keys in my hand both for my journey and those who have joined me to dare and invite His light and unlock a plan for their own life, one step at a time.

Rather than remaining in pain and staying stuck, we have the choice to welcome God into the process and, in essence, choose life anew. This becomes a veritable force of transformation. The outcome is the production of good fruit—a masterpiece drawn from productive pain, which is translated into resources for our own gain and for others.

Today, men and women who have learned these keys of putting their courage and compassion into action are building a God-given roadmap in their spheres of influence. This book offers an invitation to view various situations and relationships through the lens of risk, to look into painful wounds, and to make a prayer invitation for the light when finding a "stuck place" to welcome the possibility of something new. Transformation is possible as we take intentional steps to walk through the valley of the shadow of death because there is light on the other side.

HOW TO USE THIS BOOK AS A GUIDE

Inviting the light of God into any traumatic situation or relationship is a great first step. You won't be the first person to do this nor the last. Some very famous people, such as King David, who wrote the Psalms, believed it was important. Moses and many others from the Bible have taken this journey, and now, it's yours to receive.

Below are recommendations to gain the most benefit from this book:

- go through this book one chapter at a time

- read the scripture entry and story

- meditate on them

- ponder the question posed at the end and allow your heart to meet with God's light as a place to bring new perspectives to life's experiences

- engage in the prayers as a jumping off point

- engage in honest conversation with God the Father, Jesus the Christ, and the Holy Spirit about where you are and invite the Trinity to bring new perspectives

- God desires to give us His kingdom viewpoint—it is ours to look for it

FOUNDATIONAL SCRIPTURE AND COMMENTARY FOR THIS BOOK

"You are all children of the light and children of the day. We do not belong to the night or to the darkness."

1 THESSALONIANS 5:5 (NIV)

Today, as it has been throughout history, there are dark clouds of trouble, discord, trauma, and persecution which loom in our midst. Still, the Lord God is there and ready bring us life. As we become increasingly aware of who we are and whose we are the brilliance of His light will burst forth even brighter. The bible scripture above reminds us of this truth.

This book can help activate and advance the light of the spirit-to-spirit connection needed with our Heavenly Father God, His son Jesus Christ, and His most Holy Spirit.

In scientific terms, light breaks open as waves. As light permeates the atmosphere, it brings ever-widening facets of what has always been there. This principle translates into our original design given to us at the beginning of creation. Our life is an unfolding story to be told. The purpose and meaning of our lives are meant to be mined as a treasure waiting to be unveiled.

Although the light of our own value may seem blinding or strange at first, His presence there with you and I is able to melt away the bonds of trauma and give sight to the path forward. It's worth the journey, our destiny is still in the making. It's time to embrace the glorious Kingdom inheritance God's prepared for us, here and now.

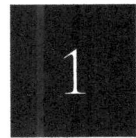

AN INVITATION

"Light-seeds are planted in the souls of God's people, joy-seeds are planted in good heart-soil."

PSALM 97:11 TM

Have you heard of seeds made from light or joy? Neither had I, but consider this, when a seed is planted into the ground it is usually very small, hard, and unassuming. The seed may be some fruit or nut, a vegetable, tree, or some other beauty of the harvest. The sower of the seed (Matthew 13:1-9) waits in great anticipation of the fulfillment of what he has planted. In nature, the seed goes through a process of transformation before becoming what is the intended planting.

Each unique seedling has a particular period of nurture in which this change is accomplished. Amidst the scruffy condition, the ground is a most unlikely place for this incubation. Yet, it is within the deep darkness, unseen to the human eye, where the elements finally will shift, crack open, and be resurrected into a dazzling design of beauty held captive by its shell.

This analogy describes what God desires to develop within our lives. Seeds of light and joy are always coming to greet us in the most unusual forms—ways that are foreign and unexpected and can be hard to recognize. It is ours to receive the gift and give a place of nurture to God's light-seed within us. This strange seed holds an unfolded treasure yet to be revealed.

What might a light-seed bring? To understand this we go to science that tells us light travels at a rate of exactly 299,792,458 meters or 983,571,056 feet per second—fast. Nothing goes as fast as light, and its properties include heat, illumination, reflection, and much more.

When God comes to pierce the darkness with His light-seeds, we can expect a breakthrough. How long has it been since there has been a significant change in your situation? Consider prayers to invite God's light as an excellent starting place. Invite it in simply by asking Him for it. Just the tiniest of openings, a crack in our shell, can usher in His extraordinary light. Seeping into the dark crevasses of the heart, His light-seeds break open fresh perspective and a renewed joy in the journey.

Question: Where is there a dark place within me where I can invite the light of God to come?

Action Prayer: God, I choose to open a place within me for You to bring Your light-seeds and transform more of my heart and life. Amen.

HIS CARE

"So when they were filled, He [Jesus] said to His disciples, 'Gather up the fragments that remain, so that nothing is lost.'"

JOHN 6:12 NKJV

Where had it come from? All this food and some left over. Not one person remained who had not eaten all their fill. Truly mind-boggling. Was it all a dream? No, remnants were being collected after the feast by the very people who, just several hours ago, were giving it all away. The people must have questioned what kind of food distribution process those followers of Jesus stumbled on.

When something so amazing and life-giving comes to us, we can find ourselves wanting to find a way to capture and duplicate it again. The astonishing, phenomenal masterpiece of this story can be hard to believe. Did it really happen? Our minds often replay the miraculous event over and over while acknowledging the unprecedented grace, generosity, and action of feeding all those people without asking a single thing in return. These types of things were unheard of on such an ordinary day by the Sea of Galilee.

Reviewing the event is not at all bad. It's important to muse over the feelings created by such extraordinary occasions within the community. The action of replaying those experiences actually builds relational connections within the brain, wiring pathways to receive and welcome positive impressions.

This process is unfamiliar and can be difficult to grasp when all you have known are repeated patterns of trauma. It takes time to train the brain to recognize and replay a positive gesture such as receiving all the food you wanted. By recalling the event, the zone where joy connections are found in the brain is strengthened. The next time positive feelings come our way it will be easier to recognize them.

The twelve baskets of food fragments left over were another incredible part of the miraculous action of feeding thousands of people with very little food. Even the scraps left behind were important to Jesus. How precious and filled with love our Lord is about what He is giving to us. He recognized and provided for the weariness and immediate need for nourishment, and the meal's remnants would keep giving for days to come. Nothing is lost when it comes from our heavenly Father's care.

Question: What provision have you been feeding on? Even the remnants, those seeming leftovers are special and worth collecting, savoring, and sharing with another.

Action Prayer: Lord, remind me of what may have seemed like a small way in which You have fed me. A remnant, some leftover which is so very valuable to You that You saw my weariness, my need for Your heavenly food. I choose to invite Your light to show me how You care and long to sustain and strengthen me. Amen.

3

UNEXPECTED GIFTS

"After some time, when he returned to get her, he turned aside to see the carcass of the lion. And behold, a swarm of bees and honey were in the carcass of the lion. He took some of it in his hands and went along, eating. When he came to his father and mother, he gave some to them, and they also ate…"

JUDGES 14:8-9 NKJV

Have you ever had one of those days when everything you touch becomes more difficult to accomplish than what you had thought it would take? Those are the kind of days when it seems like the lions are prowling around the door leading me to statements such as, "It cannot be done or, I can't do this, or this is too complex for me to tackle."

It had been a long day with more complexities to work through than there was time to complete. On those days, we need to turn with all the strength we can muster to believe that we are meant for extraordinary feats and do not have to succumb to the relentless roar of the lions surrounding us. Their assignment is to see us defeated, sent over the edge, toppling down into an abyss of self-defeat, striving in anguish over the impossibility of a situation.

Our heavenly Father's economy is not like ours. Fortunately, we can hit "reset" and redirect our perspective when we understand the fact that His resources are a gift beyond measure, available, and custom made. Does the issue feel too big? His provision is ripe for the task. These are times when we need to learn more about pushing through the pain to see the enemy defeated. We're probably stronger than we think.

Look at this portion of the verse: "after some time when he returned…" When we practice the art of receiving, acknowledging our own circumstances, and even understanding our enemies who threaten, then we'll understand how our response to adversity can literally become that which feeds us food or supply provision for the future. We must also be willing to lean into God's strength while He imparts the ability to defeat the enemy (the lion) to us!

Celebrate how the death of something can become a seedbed to bare new life and more resources. This is the principle of multiplication. It gives enough increase, enough for us and for others. We cannot outgive our heavenly Father. But as we develop a flow and connection with God, it propels us to inherit a sweet gift to feed ourselves and our family.

Question: What enemy or "lion" in your life is keeping you from living in abundance?

Action Prayer: God, there is nothing You do not see or know. I ask for Your intervention with this lion. Slay it as only You can do. I surrender to Your way to accomplish the defeat of this enemy. You are the God of life and the overcomer to the blockages. Help me to see the gift You have created out of these tribulations. Amen.

CLEARING THE PATH

"May God our Father himself and our Master Jesus clear the road to you! And may the Master pour on the love so it fills your lives and splashes over on everyone around you, just as it does from us to you. May you be infused with strength and purity, filled with confidence in the presence of God our Father when our Master Jesus arrives with all his followers."

1 THESSALONIANS 3:11-13 TM

Look at all the heavy equipment being brought in for the job of moving all the rubble and waste. I wonder where they will take it to dispose of it? When do you think they will get the job done? It's been such a long process already and such a befuddling inconvenience with the various detours required so the clearing can be completed. Such dust, mud, and debris. Can anything good come of all this? Is all the time required, effort, and cost involved really worth this process called transformation?

Perhaps, like me, you have wondered about a land project or road under construction. It so reminds me of our personal journey where God was going with all the monumental work involved in bringing our lives into some semblance of order. Will it ever produce any good? The seemingly endless piles of rubble must be moved or ground up to lay a path. This scripture points to several keys that can help to broaden our vision and steady our steps as we take the road less traveled.

The Trinity (God-Jesus-Holy Spirit) acts as a foreman whose job is to direct the plans, secure the right equipment in life, do the heavy lifting off our shoulders, and move the mountain if necessary. When we step into rhythm with the power of the Trinity, there is a sense of dominion over the situation and an ease of partnership with God in our everyday practice. The heavy yoke which hung around our neck like a chain is removed is and replaced with an infusion of confidence, strength, increased spiritual muscle, and clarity for the journey.

Gaining the momentum to clear the path and achieve renovation can be monumental and often painful. The invitation of His light along the way can show us the reserves of life-giving water which have seemed hidden to us. The feel of this light is akin to a flow of water flooding our hearts with hope, joy, and the promise of resurgence into our heart. So unlock and swing open the gates within your spirit, soul, and body to receive and build new testimonies of His glory within.

This manner of craft is demonstrated through us for our lives and those we care about. See it as the significant milestone linking to the next bend in the road, awaiting the arrival of His presence alongside you. Cherish the route to this great adventure.

Question: What path is God clearing or redefining in your life today?

Action Prayer: God, I accept this challenge to welcome Your partnership and light. I ask that You take all the broken pieces within me and form the pathway to equal the calling You have decreed for me. Demonstrate Your glory and dominion to reflect any credibility I may have earned and the good ways in which my life's journey is panning out because of the road I've traveled so far.

In loving trust, I choose to welcome the closeness of Your light to shine in and bring beauty for ashes. Give me the stamina through this painful process of clearing away what needs to be removed, and help me see amongst the rubble what is actually a gem for the journey.

Thank You for giving me Your beautiful, daily hugs of protection, direction, provision or just because I am Your child.

Help me sense and set my rhythm to Your heart's desire to shine the glorious light of Your revelation so I don't miss what is in my hand— the way marked by Your Son's payment of a high, high price. I give myself, my journey, my beginning, and my end to You. Your kingdom come and Your will be done on earth as it is in heaven. Amen.

MONDAY'S HELP

"Save me, O God, by Your name, and vindicate me by Your strength. Hear my prayer, O God; Give ear to the words of my mouth. For strangers have risen up against me, and oppressors have sought after my life; They have not set God before them. Behold, God is my helper; The Lord is with those who uphold my life. He will repay my enemies for their evil. Cut them off in Your truth. I will freely sacrifice to You; I will praise Your name, O Lord, for it is good. For He has delivered me out of all trouble; and my eye has seen its desire upon my enemies."

PSALM 54:1-7 NKJV

Light breaks in and it is the start of another day. My mind swirls and darts in and out, thinking of the possibilities another week may bring. Will this light bring something new, fresh, or lightweight for the tasks at hand? I take hold of my old, familiar cup—a symbol of the routine of drink to which I can take solace in facing the week ahead.

Then, my heart leaps as I read a page from His book. He would be my help today. Monday, the God of heaven and earth says to me that He will defend, hear, hold me up to His light, and be a rescuer from traps conspired against me.

Grabbing hold of this strengthens me to the core. The someone coming for me is God Himself, and He will cause me to know the day as He sees it. I can welcome this Monday morning as a holy sight, as He makes my blind eyes to see like Him because He is with me.

Question: Is God still there on Mondays?

Action Prayer: Lord, You know the dimensions, ways, and desperation of my heart. Break into these well-worn pathways I have carved out that have become so dull and ordinary. My spirit longs to live out of what You have called the "great adventure." Break me free from the traps laid for me by the enemy, and release me from the "ordinary" to the "edge" that You sparked within. Here is my day; I lay it at Your feet to own. Only let me steward it in such a way to fan the fire of true purpose, desire, and kingdom living. Amen.

6

EYES TO SEE

"Tell me where you're working —I love you so much—Tell me where you're tending your flocks, where you let them rest at noontime. Why should I be the one left out, outside the orbit of your tender care?"

SONG OF SOLOMON 1:7 TM

The struggle is real, and where there is a sense of not belonging, it can be tempting to run and hide. This is similar to trying to protect ourselves by going away and intentionally draping ourselves with grave clothes. A sense of desperation and heightened fear adds to the mayhem. The struggle leaves us ruled by the very things we were meant to have dominion over. Perhaps a compulsion or obsessive behavior takes hold, increasing the trauma seared on the soul. How far away the dream and promise of true inheritance feels at this point.

In this pivotal moment of internal struggle, we can either expand our view or turn our eyes away down some narrow, unadventurous, myopic road. It is how we respond in our most anxious moments to determine our field of vision and scope of understanding for now and the future.

Choosing to grow and not retreat during times of desperation takes courage and tenacity. When we choose to expand, God comes along to help us recognize and receive something new. It is His loving desire to meet us there in the place of our greatest need. We can apply these principles when we feel our vision begin to dim.

It starts by resisting the "shut down," which most times shows itself as a sense of being lost in an unfamiliar place, separated, distracted, and even overwhelmed. After resisting, press in. Receive the light of God's presence and deliberately welcome Him to come and give you the ability to revive and rebound. Last, breathe in and allow your senses to delight in His being there with you.

Allow yourself to feel the expansion as He caresses your human spirit and grounds it to His own. Take care not to sacrifice the savor of these instances amidst the longing for some momentary relief.

> **Question:** Where is God asking you to expand your vision?

Action Prayer: God, I choose to receive and drink deeply from Your reservoir of strength as a divine invitation and daily discipline in these times when I'm tempted to run and hide. I choose You and this long-awaited cup of cold water to refresh and restore me along this cracked and weary journey.

As an act of my will, I open my human spirit, welcome Your life-giving light, and choose to treasure the refreshment of Your presence as a fountain of life that will never run dry. I ask You to teach me how to engage regularly and create many entry points of intimate connection with You, God. Amen.

7

A LANDING PLACE

"God is in her palaces; He is known as her refuge."

PSALM 48:3 NKJV

Where do you go when the presence of God seems far and distant? What I've discovered is He's right there where I last found Him. All I had to do was return to that point.

Our own personal entry points, promoting quietness within ourselves, and giving room to connect more closely with God. Wherever that place may be—where it's safe, peaceful, and you feel cared for—is where His comforting presence comes to meet you. Why? Our God and His Son, the Lord Jesus Christ, exist outside of time and space, and His eternal desire is to be with us always.

Developing an open space within ourselves, let's learn to make use of gratitude in everyday moments which prepare a landing place to rest in God. All told, creating that internal platform for our peaceful refuge is up to us.

Take a deep breath and quiet yourself. Examine the territory of your heart and celebrate those glimpses of appreciation that come your way in the ordinary everyday ways. By cultivating this daily practice of acknowledgement and gratefulness, you'll soon find a haven in the making. Next, look around your internal landing place and see where the Lord comes in. For Deuteronomy 31:8 (NKJV) says, "...He will not leave you nor forsake you..."

We find a safe refuge by placing one block of grace and gratitude upon another. This investment takes work, time, and effort on our part, but the result is joy.

Take notice of the trail of occasions where you've received some sign of joy. Savor the small stuff—a flower in blossom, a gentle smile, a child's laughter, or a well-worn machine that faithfully works. It could be the tiniest thing. Savor them. Now tuck each one into your heart and recount them at the end of the day as a special gift.

These building blocks of joy will become your sanctuary and refuge of consecration from which love and time can flow in rhythm with your King of Glory, the One who is a true and just defender and victor over all things.

Question: Where have you added a deeper place of landing for you and God to meet?

Action Prayer: Lord, help me to have eyes to see the ways You arrange beauty and sparkles of Your love to come alongside me. As an act of my will, I choose to catch glimpses of Your generosity as the precious blessings they are. Bring Your light to my spirit, soul, heart, and body so I can live in an unbroken flood of joy. Lord, You have planned this divine refuge of rest for me that I might rest in You. Amen.

IN THE MIDST, HE IS HERE

"God is in the midst of her, she shall not be moved;
God shall help her, just at the break of dawn."

PSALM 46:5 NKJV

While trying to navigate the pandemic trauma blanketing the global community, I stumbled onto something new related to rest. It was as if the pursuit of my faith required a new level of expression—a way to come alive with freshness.

Wouldn't you know it! Just as the shadows begin to loom, threatening to gobble us up, would just so happen to coincide with the need for us to start exercising deeper connections with God, anyway? So many times, the picture I had painted for myself typically wound up adding even more bars to a self-imposed prison. But this time, I choose the road less traveled to transport me outside the limits of these surrounding human conditions. And this is what I found:

The God of heaven and earth sits right here, with me in the middle of the brokenness. His enormous love and delight are with me. His type of love is the glue when all else becomes unstuck. How many times have I failed to recognize the lasting imprint of His hand that power beyond my own, which has held me together one more time? That gentle breeze, the soft, sweet birdsong, and the kaleidoscope of colors dashed across the sky in a most audacious display of creation's call. And for what purpose, you ask? To speak to me and all mankind, heralding His glorious presence is here.

His utter joy is to share the spectacle of His attendance with us through His tenacious care of each detail. Each facet of life intertwines and builds a more solid stage for God's plan. I release my care to His never-ending ability to lead. Even in my weariness, an unseen link holds me fast and keeps my wavering at bay.

Question: Where, in your experience of trauma, do you need to see God's presence?

Action Prayer: Thank you, God, for it is You who will come. Help me to know You are present as You fashion relief for me from this condition—an emergence intended for my good. May I return to the refuge of Your love which bids me to come. Forgive my reservations. Forge for me weapons of relentless light to shine through as a reflection of Your pleasure and Your reward. Your kingdom come as it is in Heaven. Amen.

9

THE HOUR HAS COME

"Jesus spoke these words, lifted up His eyes to heaven, and said: 'Father, the hour has come. Glorify Your Son, that Your Son also may glorify You.'"

JOHN 17:1 NKJV

Leaving a residue in the earth or a mark of distinction behind is something most of us hope to someday accomplish. Whether it's imparting wisdom to someone, a parcel of land, a bequeath of money, or giving any part of ourselves to another when we die is both selfless and life-giving—for both the "will-maker" to give and the "beneficiary" to receive. It's a utilitarian process when someone leaves a will as a sign of their legacy to a relative or friend. Be it material or monetary, chances are, the inherited assets probably took a lifetime for the will-maker to acquire.

This legacy is often a true vestige of love and the means by which the giver passes on a bit of themself.

In this verse, Jesus is imparting a similar treasure as He says to God, the Father, "The hour has come. Glorify Your Son, that Your Son also may glorify You." These words are often read as part of some larger, more meaty application of the story, but in this instance, we'll look at the less obvious message in this single phrase.

From a flow of oneness with His heavenly Father, Jesus receives the gift of birthright and history is forever changed. Out of the place of relationship, surrender, and intimacy between Christ and His heavenly Father, a whole new level of fulfillment is born for mankind.

This chapter also speaks of the legacy Jesus left to us as His disciples. Like them, we may be wondering what will come next for us at this critical point in time. How out of control His original disciples must have felt, unsure of what would come next. In turn, we might be asking ourselves what new kind of yielding will this undiscovered territory require of us?

This is our inheritance, and we must take hold of it with all its rough and unrefined edges. As proponents of this scripture, we can resist temptations to wish it was different or had come at a more convenient time.

This is the hour of an inheritance transfer, and it is our time to receive it enthusiastically. Proverbs 25:2 (NKJV) says, "*It is the glory of God to conceal a matter, but the glory of kings is to* search out a matter." (Emphasis added).

Question: Is there a treasure God has placed in your life, and is He asking you to take hold and accept?

Action Prayer: Jesus, You modeled true unity of relationship with Your heavenly Father. Honor and respect are the hallmarks of Your oneness. I welcome Your light to create an open space within me to receive all of the ways my inheritance is to come.

Whether it's through relationship, under certain conditions or situations, give me Your grace to rest as You show me how to mine the riches of heaven. Thank You for what You have given me—a place in You for me to grow in strength and determination, to dig deeply, and resist turning away from the treasure within. Amen.

10

AN UNUSUAL WORK

"For the Lord will rise up as at Mount Perazim, He will be angry as in the Valley of Gibeon—That He may do His work, His awesome work, and bring to pass His act, His unusual act."

ISAIAH 28:21 NKJV

We live in what has been called "unprecedented times." Our population is varied in its stance on a range of issues, from politics to long-term weather patterns. Today, society is filled with anticipation of what will come next and pleads for hope and assurance. But as this verse tells us, there's always been an element of the unusual in God's economy.

For now, let your human spirit stir with a hopeful outlook as God unfolds how He wants to do business in our lives. Rising up "as at Mount Perazim," mentioned in this verse, was a place where the newly crowned King David had defeated the enemy, the Philistines. That may sound ordinary to you unless you've studied the conditions of that day and what surrounded him.

David and his men fell into full combat as the entire Philistine nation had "deployed themselves" to a nearby Jerusalem valley in ready expectation of war. In verse 18, David gets away from the camp so he might check in with God as to the next plan of action. He sought God's advice only to hear Him say, "He would deliver the enemy into David's hands" as he went into battle. Next, still at Mount Perazim, David wrote his new understanding of the character of God as Master of Breakthrough.

Sometimes it seems exhausting to take time out to intentionally check in with the Lord. Perhaps like me, you have thought, *He has so much already, and will He really shed light on my situation?* Yet, it means everything when we hear just one word, a direction, instruction, assurance, provision, or divine strategy in a time of crisis.

It's in these times of upheaval when God loves to reveal His unusual work. Let's not miss unwrapping the gift of His work to bring additional light.

Question: Where do you need God's deliverance and breakthrough strategy?

Action Prayer: Lord, I proclaim You the master of breakthrough! Crown my thoughts with a heavenly understanding that I am Your child and joint-heir with Christ. Hear my call to receive the truth about this battle and Your destiny. When it is time to cross over into the next level and possess my birthright, Lord, I choose to look to You for strategies. Show me the components and key resources deposited within and around me and how to use them to keep in step with Your ways and unusual work. Amen.

CARRY ME OUT

"He also brought me up out of a horrible pit, out of the miry clay, and set my feet upon a rock, and established my steps."

PSALM 40:2 NKJV

Finding ourselves in deep strife often plants us fair and square in what seems the most impossible and vacuous position, a hard place to find a foothold out. It's as though the world starts caving in and any window of opportunity to escape the anguish becomes so narrow we can barely see the light at the end—making for an ideal environment to fight, flight, or freeze in response.

We all can attest to times like those described in the (above) verse. Getting into trouble is as easy as slipping down a wet and icy hill. The tough part is getting back up.

The shock and sudden awareness of finding trouble on our doorstep can be overwhelming, painfully slow to process, and demoralizing. In terms of my own experiences, I now recognize how extremely cautious I've become having hit a few slippery slopes of my own. Inching forward, one foot in front of the other, looking for a secure patch to place my next step and get a grip, I usually find the only thing to hold onto is my faith.

What I'm finding along the journey is where there's unexpected trouble there lies a deep well of gratitude on the other side. More recently, I'm pleased to say, my heart is learning to slow down and enjoy how God directs me in a number of new and uplifting ways through turmoil and trouble. What about you? Can you sense how God longs to lift you up and out by His own hand and place your steps onto a more solid foundation?

Notice the first two places where David found himself in this verse—in a pit and miry clay. Both are anything but stable. But like David, we are meant to receive a way out. Consider God's faithfulness to meet us at the point of our greatest need. He knows what is best for us and guides us to that steady foothold. This calls for abounding gratitude and joyous recognition of a well-designed plan to guide us to higher ground.

Question: What is your response when trouble comes your way? Could it be the Lord's doing?

Action Prayer: Hear my invitation to You, Lord, to come into this time of trouble and shine Your light into the darkness. May this trouble springboard me into new solidarity with the testimony of my life from a place of Your grace. I choose to be grateful for Your steadfast love that is ready to guide and establish my going out and coming in. Amen.

12

REVEALING HIMSELF

"Hear my prayer, O Lord, and give ear to my cry; do not be silent at my tears; for I am a stranger with You. A sojourner, as all my fathers were. Remove Your gaze from me, that I may regain strength, before I go away and am no more."

PSALM 39:12-13 NKJV

Lord, how many times have I come with uncertain prayers to make a request to You? At first, I pleaded, only to become familiar with my own tears and hearing the sobs of disappointment or some saddened condition I found myself in. Without first going through the complexities of filtering out the truth from the lies I believed, I have no point of access to reach You. There is no automatic open door for prayers.

Broken and lost, I cry out towards heaven in hopes of a drink of Your gaze toward me. Recognizing my own needs compels me to venture close, modestly ask for an audience before You, the King, in this most holy place.

How remarkable! The door flings open, and I am basking in the beauty which flows down and over me by no endeavor of my own. You, the supreme maker of the universe, coming through dimensions of time and space to encounter me! That longed-for prayer answered, and in Your presence, I'm in awe and oblivious to the content of my own request.

For You are here, it is You and through the blood that a covenant of Your Son's agreement of adoption is stamped upon my heart. We are together. My tears do not obstruct Your view of me, nor the stinging discomfort of their presence. Every part of me is humbled as there is no turning from Your loving stare upon me.

Such love and sheer loveliness of Your presence flow over my utter depravity. Now exposed by this blinding light of Yours, I am undone. I'm without words or manner of gifts worthy of such nobility. But I must ask one more thing of You. With trembling lips, I ask, "Could You remove Your gaze from me? Though grieved with sorrow for the asking, the brilliance of Your glory has brought me to my knees." I didn't believe it possible to survive under such weight of glory.

In an instant, Your hand lifts, and I arise, forever seared by the mark of Your presence fashioned in my core. Beneath me now and new to my sight is an exquisite gem with hues of blue set as a milestone in my path, evidence of this most sacred journey. You have come and unlocked the door to the chamber to all my desires.

Question: Where in your world could you pray to invite God to show you His presence?

Action Prayer: Lord, there is nowhere I can go from Your presence, yet the intensity of my days can sometimes overwhelm me. I so need to see You. I choose to make You a priority. Redeem the time as I surrender my day to You. Cause me to hunger and thirst for the light and reality of Your desire to shine through me today in a variety of ways. Amen.

13

BURDENS TOO HEAVY

"For Your arrows pierce me deeply, and Your hand presses me down. There is no soundness in my flesh because of Your anger, nor any health in my bones because of my sin. For my iniquities have gone over my head; like a heavy burden they are too heavy for me. My wounds are foul and festering because of my foolishness."

PSALM 38:2-5 NKJV

Beloved, God chastises those whom He loves. There are times when we are called to reflect on areas not previously known and to recognize our part which has brought our heart such sorrow.

Consider this example: A cute quote or snappy limerick was shared with you. Now, time goes on and you begin to repeat it to others, this time as if it were yours. It's a casual offense, easy to gloss over the fact that it came from someone else. Does this minor incident cause our Lord a frown of disdain?

I have known that frown and come to heartfelt tears by this example in three ways:

1. This was a careless degradation of the person's value, who originally created the quote.

2. By repeating someone else's words as my own, there was an agreement with a lie. A belief that what I had to say was not valuable or clever enough. This causal agreement leaves me with a feeling of being less adequate than someone else.

3. The action declared to my own heart that the work of God was doing within me was insufficient. YUCK!

The words we utter, whether written or verbal, are part of the framework of our witness or testimony to the world. When we can see how we are fashioned by God, there comes an increased ability to steward our place in right order to how the story in our history will change the world. Our story has been given to us to both experience and invite His tale of redemption and glory to be told through us.

I have seen His delight when by recognition and repentance I've come to know where I got off track and as the verse tells "the heavy burden is too much for me." God means these acknowledgements to be too heavy because He longs for us to know Him and our desperate need for Him in our lives. The continued work of Christ, His beloved Son, and forgiveness is found in the choice to let His light show what part is mine and lay those burdens down at His feet.

Question: Where can you invite His light to show you what you've been missing?

Action Prayer: Lord, I come to You as one in need. Forgive me, Lord, for the way in which I have defiled my brethren by taking something which was not mine. Forgive me for hurting Your heart by agreeing with Your enemy that what I have and who I am is not sufficient for a testimony.

Forgive me for agreement with lies and for grieving Your heart. I stand in Your court and plead guilty. Jesus, You alone are sufficient. Please come and take this trash to Your cross? Cover my guilt with Your holy blood. May my part be dealt a death blow. Cut me free from any unholy alliance and bring my spirit, soul, and body into right alignment and reconciliation in every part of my being. Amen.

14

EATING BEAUTY

"Trust in the Lord, and do good; dwell in the land and feed on His faithfulness."

PSALM 37:3 NKJV

There are four actions specified within this single verse that, when acted upon, unlock a fresh and new understanding of His sovereignty and how we interact with it. These actions are trust, do good, dwell in the land, and feed. In Scripture, the number four represents the triune God, Father, Son, and Holy Spirit (the Trinity), plus the fourth, the Kingdom of God here on earth, otherwise known as the Church. When one of these identities is blocked, the symptoms behave like the human heart. Where there's a blockage, there becomes a resulting pain, lack of rhythm, and ripple effect that impacts the other three from flowing strong and freely.

How about God's goodness? Were you able to remain secure in mind and heart, believing the pain and unexpected turns in the road would bring you to a just and righteous conclusion? Go a step further and ask, "Heart, can you rest in the current situation, condition, and way in which relationships are placed around you?" Consult again with your personal spirit, "Is it well with my soul?" And lastly, do you see any shadows of misperception blocking you from feeding on God's devotion to you?

Consider the times you willingly or unwillingly were dependent on God or someone else to come through for you in a meaningful way, and they did. Allow the memories to surface and make a note of them for future reference. Invite Holy Spirit to seed these positive memories deep within the foundations of your grid for trust.

Remember those seasons when an extraordinary phone call, meeting, or invitation was given to you with no preconceived knowledge or attempt on your part. Recall and savor the wonder and glorious gratitude that filled your heart. Invite those emotions to come and infuse your personal spirit now again with the hope of His goodness.

Next, marinate on the gift of God's presence in the very place you awoke to today. Drink it in and allow the exultant sensations of His presence to arise within and sing. The glory of the Lord is here in the land of the living, and He is WITH YOU and watches over you.

Finally, precious spirit, be nourished and encouraged for the meager meal you have brought with you that you thought wouldn't go very far; it has been set before the sovereign King over heaven and earth. This sustenance, when DIVIDED and shared, can now feed you as well as your family, community, and the entire region of hungry ones. Celebrate what was multiplied at His banqueting table. Your partnership with Him is a banner of His love over you.

Question: Is there a blockage that impedes your ability to receive in any of these four areas?

Action Prayer: I invite You, Holy Spirit, to incorporate this bread of faithfulness into my framework and bring the cumulative record of all the righteous actions in my life found in these four chambers of treasure. Embed these gifts deep within this fresh, clean structure of my human spirit. Help me build again and learn to savor a new language being custom created for the unique design given to me by the One who adores and knows me through and through. Amen.

15

THE TANGY TASTE OF GOODNESS

"Oh, taste and see that the LORD is good; Blessed is the man who trusts in Him!"

PSALM 34:8 NKJV

No more edits. This is a time for truth and coming to terms with all the terms our heavenly Father has set before us today. Let me be the decision-maker who's ready to stand and be counted! No longer swayed by adverse breezes flowing over the land, I now secure my position knowing our King, the Lord of heaven and earth, is here!

Situations will ebb and flow, but our God stands resolute and unswerving. Heaven's manifesto is breaking forth in this hour for the culmination of His glory to be revealed. Take note of this day and very hour. He's sending a declaration of His Word as to what must go and what is to stay. Do not hesitate to put your matters in order so there may be an alignment and a release of the virtue God has placed within you to flow over and bless the earth.

Question: How are you positioned to receive the Lord of heaven and earth? Where do you stand?

Action Prayer: Lord, I welcome Your wisdom to help with the choices set before me in all situations, opportunities, and relationships. You are a good Father, and there's no time or inclination for compromise or caveats now. You have called me to align with Your plans because the sacrifice was already made.

Here at the altar of your gift, King Jesus the Christ, I ask Your guidance and extended favor to multiply the resources within me and be made holy by Your hand. I give ownership to You of all that I am and all I have. Lord of the Universe, I choose to take responsibility to maintain what

You call and entrust me to carry. I accept and make room for this heavenly partnership with You and to follow in step with Your heart toward this massive love You have shown me. Amen.

16

HE HEARS

"They looked to Him and were radiant, and their faces were not ashamed. This poor man cried out, and the Lord heard him, and saved him out of all his troubles."

PSALM 34:5-6 NKJV

God longs to be a part of every aspect of our life story from the most crippling of conditions to the most magnificent successes. He's the proudest Dad any child could ever have.

As individuals, we're not so easy on ourselves compared to God's viewpoint of us. Trying to understand our neediness and depravity doesn't have to involve a self-deprecating dialogue with ourselves about some great loss. On the contrary, it can present an opportunity to demonstrate our most noble conviction as we turn to find Him for guidance. Observe how the very essence of us transforms into His likeness in the presence of the One who transcends time, space, and every dimension.

Having troubles are part of our life's journey. Engaging with God in the middle of our issues provides us with an on-ramp to the expressway where we can merge back into line in our relationship with Him. It starts when sharing all our feelings candidly.

When we become honest with where we are in our trauma, His light can find its way in through the cracks. There in the middle of our heart's cry, joy begins to shine. God is always waiting and at the ready to hear the cry of His child calling for Him.

Question: What is the cry of your heart today and are you willing to share it with God?

Action Prayer: Oh, heavenly Father, I choose to call out to You and ask You to answer and be here with me in this place. Will You do whatever is required to bring transformation to this situation, place, or circumstance? I'm so glad You do not mind and can handle all my pain. I am honored and willing to make room for You to come and reveal Your Father's heart of love to me. Thank You for hearing me, being available, and saving the very best for me in times I need it the most. Amen.

17

HE IS HERE

"Do not harden your hearts, as in the rebellion, as in the day of trial in the wilderness, when your fathers tested Me; they tried Me, though they saw My work."

PSALM 95:8-11 NKJV

There's no weakness in having a time-out to nurture your personal spirit with some tenderness. The key is what we hold ourselves to in times of the busy unknown, when we can't see future outcomes. Are we afraid we'll somehow wind up losing something if we take a break from it? This is the oldest deception in the book—look what happened in the Garden of Eden. Today, I think we use the acronym, FOMO or "fear of missing out."

There are times in all our lives when keeping up the constant pace can become too much. We might find ourselves feeling particularly raw after a tough week, for instance, or after a long-drawn-out situation that carried a great deal of trauma related to family or a loved one. It could be anything to burn us out. And here's where we need to take time to stop, rest, and recharge.

Where do you go in those times to rest? Do you recharge in God's embrace or become preoccupied with some distraction? Any one of us can be distracted from a place of intentional rest, quiet, and feeding of the personal spirit. Sometimes, it's just hard to slow down. In such cases, we'll do well to ensure we're not substituting our place of rest with alternate places to cover up.

Question: Do you need your eyes opened to something particular, today?

Action Prayer: Jesus, I ask You for a release of fresh grace from Your Spirit to help focus on the situation set before me. This wilderness is not unseen by You. I call my personal spirit to listen so these words, thoughts, and deeds set before fuel for a transformation to my inner person.

Lord, show me Your heart and the signs for this journey. Dismantle structures of darkness that have dimmed my vision of who You really are. I choose to lock my sights on Your heavenly light and plan. Join me with Your presence, King of kings, Jesus by spirit, soul, and body. I choose to set some quiet time as a priority in this moment. May Your existence hold my heart steady, so when it's time, I will sense the strong and gentle leading of Your heavenly hand guiding me through the next turn in the road. Amen.

18

A HIDDEN GEM

"I will extol You, O Lord, for You have lifted me up, and have not let my foes rejoice over me."

PSALM 30:1 NKJV

There are two key points to consider about how we respond when receiving bad news. First, we might establish an overall picture of the incident and what's so "bad" about it. And while we figure that out, we start wondering how we feel about the occurrence and how it makes us feel inside. Getting or giving someone bad news is unsettling for both sides of the information exchange, so the topic starts raising questions. Then, receiving the bad news brings up memories from the past where there was a similar loss of something or someone. All this, and it was only a minute ago you received the bad news. If only we could practice our ability to simply observe the receipt of bad news and move through the mental processes a bit differently, getting bad news might not have to be so shocking.

The second point to consider is equally complex and pivotal to our response to receiving bad news. This component requires an intentional focus on the face value of the news itself. This alleviates becoming stuck in processing the pain or any shadows of memory to remind us of the past. This is where the connection between the brain and spirit may need more practice in developing new pathways, as described in the verse (above).

Let's look at the word David uses in the first verse of "A Psalm and Song at the Dedication of the House of David." He refers to "extol." The word extol carries a rich meaning for those who are in the midst of accepting bad news. It speaks of a willingness not to turn away but towards our heavenly King for help. This is not the usual direction we tend to track toward and requires a large amount of intentionality on our part. Of the many dictionary listings online and in hardback, the word also means to lift up, praise to the skies, and to give room.[1]

When we ponder the word "room," it can depict several meanings that also include a reference to some sort of space or making space (give room) to a place of work, sleep, eating, a place to gather, or play. An expansion of the word room invites further interpretation. To receive bad news and make room, we must understand what we are making room for spatially. This is where a new pattern possibly emerges. This room might actually serve as a place for wisdom, insight, and considerations outside of our own limited experience or expectation. Perhaps this is what will keep us from getting stuck in the emotional pain of bad news and assist us in growing. The possibilities are endless.

Here's a mind-picture to help expand our imaginations—it is like finding a diamond buried at the bottom of a foxhole we've leapt into to escape enemy fire. In the foxhole, a gem is worthless unless something changes or someone jumps in with us. Otherwise, there's not a whole lot of use for a gem there in a hole. Discovering a diamond can only be life changing when we: 1) recognize what it is, 2) can remove it from that spot to somewhere new, or 3) know where to go to exchange it for something of value.

Question: Is there a place to make room for what might be buried treasure or a blessing in a situation where you have received bad news?

Action Prayer: King of Glory, we make room for You in the midst of this or any horrendous news. Thank you for sending a discovery, new perspective, instruction, or different set of tools to us as we find ourselves in this place.

Add Your dimensional shield of life to bad news situations and show us the gem hidden in the hole where we have taken cover. May the enemy of our King Jesus have no victory because we refuse to give it to him. Come Lord into everything and give me Your wisdom and piercing light to see the gemstone that has been here with me to cause me to grow up. Amen.

19

UNTIE ME LORD

"Pull me out of the net which they have secretly laid for me, for You are my strength."

PSALM 31:4 NKJV

A modern-day Robin Hood in his time, warrior, empire builder, purported slayer of Goliath, political figure, poet, hymnodist, local hero, wanted man, husband of several wives, and father to nineteen children, by all accounts, David, King of Israel and Judah, was a popular fellow who had a lot on his plate. It stands to reason that while he made many friends, he had more than his fair share of enemies as well—God NOT being one of them. Quite the opposite, as we've come to learn through books of the Old Testament, David was also best known for his resolute sincerity, great convictions, and relationship with God. David turned to God in times of good and bad, as depicted in the verse where he makes an emotional plea to His King and Lord, praying for a rescue out of the "net which they have secretly laid for me…"

Often, we can become self-reliant, relying on our ability to take notice of our immediate situation or surroundings for the sake of survival. So it should follow that our instincts to act and react in this world are, in part, what has helped keep us afloat. Imagine when we find ourselves "caught up" in a sticky web of conflict or a network of entanglement. Whether it happens literally or figuratively, life's variety of knots and loops can find us feeling trapped and snarled as a captured animal snared in a net. Life's variety of knots come in all sorts of configurations of fouled entanglements, such as relational interactions, workplace deadlines, family dynamics, psychological, personal, financial, or loss, to mention a few.

When the net ever entangles, you and I might very well find ourselves going round and round only to return right back to where we started. Do we surrender or fight harder? My experience has shown me to do neither. Instead, if I slow down and inspect each knot at its core, I'm able to, with God's light, carefully unravel the mess and find the strength to be restored. Taking the time to focus on each "knot" as it appears to us allows for intentional time to contemplate and, in some instances, causes the subsequent kinks to dissolve away. This simple success can bring a place of rest, relief, and new perspectives.

Question: What is at the core of the knots that seem to be holding you back?

Action Prayer: Lord, You see my tangled mess. I choose to lay the knots at Your feet while I trust in Your care and delight that pulls me out of this web as I allow Your light to shine on each knot. Turn me back towards You in this pain and blanket me with the glimmer of hope. Hold me close, as I understand my part which has brought me here. Show me You, my strong tower and Savior. Strengthen me to cast away sorrow as I see yet another knot. Teach me how another snarl can become an opportunity in Your economy. I put my confidence in You, the One who cannot fail. Amen.

20

LIFTER OF MY HEAD

"Such is the generation of those who seek him, who seek your face, God of Jacob. Lift up your heads, you gates; be lifted up, you ancient doors, that the King of glory may come in."

PSALM 24:6-7 NIV

Are you among the people described in this verse? This brings to mind a painting I saw in a museum many years ago by Pieter Paul Rubens called The Israelites Gathering Manna in the Desert, created in 1626. What struck me most was the portrayal of the characters in their various states of activity in what appeared to be a bustling scene of carrying head-baskets of food, small white matter falling from the clouds, and Moses and a young girl looking skyward.

There were a couple of men (one of whom is Moses), women, and children in close proximity to one another, each looking grateful, content, and happy. Their focus was the gathering of food or the edible "manna," which prevented them from certain starvation. Manna is made from insect droppings. These white drops were found on stems of shrubs and are the digestive byproducts of insects that feed on the plant's sap, known as honeydew. The secretion forms at night when the liquid hardens to form sweet white granules. Apparently, manna tastes like wafers made with honey. Its shelf life is only one day. The so-called "man-hu" or manna literally means "what is it?"[2] These ancient pilgrims, by now called Israelites, were on their forty-fifth or so day of wandering through the Sinai Desert after leaving Egypt.

In stark contrast to everyone else in the painting, Moses held his arms uplifted toward heaven and, amid the dire need of these weary immigrants, stood in grace, inspiration, and faith as instructed by God. The Lord had promised Moses it would "rain bread from heaven" to feed the people. Low and behold, after the next morning's layer of dew fell around camp, a precious life-saving gift. Moses shared his story about the manna and told the people to eat as much as they liked or needed.

In the painting, he is looking not towards the baskets of manna but to the heavens. Filled with a knowledge of God from his own experience, Moses is a model example of those who would lift their eyes to the giver, Jehovah Jireh (Genesis 22:14 NIV), the Lord who is our powerful provider who will lead the way through the times of the unknown.

Question: What are your eyes looking towards?

Action Prayer: Heavenly Father, I lift my eyes to You. I desire to be among the generation who seek Your face and not Your hand. You are the God who with each breaking dawn fills creation with resounding echoes of love and brings congruence between us in extravagant ways. My wildest dreams cannot compare with what You have designed for me. You will sustain me.

I am coming to recognize the beauty and sophistication of assets deposited all around me. Although I may need refinement and correction to focus with a new lens for this assimilation, I agree with Your heart to give me a land filled with the raw materials of promise.

Yes, the Savior of the world, Christ the King, has secured the victory and has all dominion. Now, I look up and see it is You, the hinge pin of the gates waiting for me. I speak to my personal spirit to swing wide and open these ancient gates and receive the dispensation of power and authority essential to occupy the land of the King's service. Amen.

HE IS GOOD

"Surely your goodness and love will follow me all the days of my life, and I will dwell in the house of the Lord forever."

PSALM 23:6 NIV

Where can I go from Your Spirit? The awe of God's goodness is a place of nurturing and a settlement of peace. Thanks be to God for a place of surrender and intimate knowledge of the Eternal One. He pursues each of us with passionate desire.

It's time to lay those things we hold dear down at His feet. Only through our release can the truth come and shine through with the single vision necessary to walk in transformation. God is not finished with you as some of us say. Listen to the silence, and in your heart return to your heavenly Father's house. There you will find the fullness of life.

Question: Ask yourself, what is it that I hold true and believe about God?

Action Prayer: Call me, Lord, to more of You and fulfill Your intent in me and the investment of my longing to awaken in every area of my life. Let the music of creation bring a fresh revelation and new stirring within as I seek to understand this time of suffering as redeemable because of Your love for me.

There is a refrain, as there is within music, a recurring pattern. Lord, may all manner of heavenly assets that are mine be readily available and at my disposal. Teach me how to see, receive, and use these tools as Your noble subject. I choose to completely unpack, know, and learn from these well-suited gifts given to me for the journey. It is Your good pleasure to give me the Kingdom of God here on earth as it is in heaven, and my reward is with You, alone. Fill me up to overflowing with this resounding truth. Amen.

22

THE TABLE IS SET

"You prepare a table before me in the presence of my enemies. You anoint my head with oil; my cup overflows."

PSALM 23:5 NIV

A table is prepared for you and me. The history of kitchen tables, reaching back through the generations to the biblical days, indicate they were first made of wood and alabaster in their construction. In that era, a table made of wood represented the delicate nature of our humanity, while the alabaster mosaic inlays carefully crafted into the table design showed a mark of distinction at a great cost.

Such a worthy "table" was demonstrated to me in my mother's final days of life, as she lay preparing to donate her organs after being pronounced brain dead at the age of sixty-three. Having spent most of her life running in fear, her closing years were the unleashing of her destiny as one who knew the sweet peace of the greatest lover of all, Christ.

Moving out of decades of addiction into a celebration of freedom, Mother had come to know Him and was reconciled across generations, cultures, and people groups the world over. Lying on this table in the presence of her enemy, death, it was the King of Kings Himself who called the final shots and proclaimed the verdict as the Author and Finisher of her faith.

One by one, family gathered. It became apparent those of us present had not assembled collectively since the time of the "great divorce" many years prior. Each one received Mother on their own turf over those final five years as she traveled the world over to offer the gift of her authenticity and reconciliation.

Each of those folks now stood rallied around the bed as a miracle salve continued to pour forth. With resounding thanks, many arrived at her bedside to testify how Mother's life with her language of authenticity had been lived out before them and had come to touch them in some influential way, giving a much-needed infusion of courage for their own journey.

Medical processes continued and still others came. Little ones, big ones, poor, rich, and every variation in between shared their experience. All were able to witness one's passing over a threshold, from a place of dark dedication to one fulfilled in their God-given design. There was no doubt, the Lord was there releasing tears of joy down every cheek and into the waiting cups of love for each one to drink.

Question: What has been brought to the table in your life?

Action Prayer: I choose to take heart and present what has been brought to the table in my life to You. Through times of duress, help me see how You are transcending across dimensions to connect my story with Your majestic alliance to bring a feast of life to myself and others. Thank You for lifting me up and across.

This table is set, and Your grand ceremony and faithful power I employ to defeat all things contrary to Your intents and purposes in my life. Holy Spirit, help me to rest in bowed grace with folded hands to be Your servant as Your plans unfold at the table. Bring Your light to help guide me, to see how this table is a gift reserved for me as I willingly take my seat at this threshold of glory. Amen.

23

HOLD FAST

"Even though I walk through the darkest valley, I will fear no evil, for you are with me; your rod and your staff, they comfort me."

PSALM 23:4 NIV

Some seasons and relationships may seem insurmountable to navigate simply because they're often complex in nature and typically in a continual state of flux. The only variable that remains constant in the equation is change. Finding the confidence to take a fearless approach to confront various types of change presents its own challenges, in some situations, seemingly death-defying. This applies in many forms, such as the death of a promise, vision, dream, hope, plan, relationship, or even the end of life of someone greatly loved.

Walking through any of these dark, shadowy prospects can catapult us into a deep ravine of despair. Alternately, denying change is not the answer. It's critical we examine our present selves in order to absorb all the lessons we're meant to receive at this moment in time. Secondly, as the verse represents, we must continue to walk *through* this valley of change against any oncoming gale winds of fear.

Question: Since change is inevitable, how are you leaning in?

Action Prayer: Lord, in places when I cannot see, I cry out to You. Your presence is the absolute best way for me to know I am Your top priority. Whatever it takes, I will stop, drop, or even crawl to Your feet, so I can touch the hem of Your garment and find those shoes of the gospel of peace today. Blanket me within with reconciliation and quiet my heart as I pass through this dell of darkness.

Crown me with rulership of authority, righteousness, and impartation from the seed bed of blessings You desire for this and coming generations. You are consecrating us as Yours, and it is my blessing to receive. When I recognize a secret place of purposeful pain, help me endure knowing it's Your mark of love and courage being etched with Your own design upon my heart.

Move my vision from the valley to the other side, so I may know the positive stance and unending endurance You require of me in the middle of the enemy's scheme. I choose to step out with vigor as if to flex the muscles of will through Your power to prepare for the next necessary and right action. I will defy personal comfort and embrace You as my Heavenly Father, along with any needed correction, so Your joy may be made full within me.

I speak to my personal spirit to call out and invite Your light of inspection in every situation where You call me to avoid compromise. I am coming to now understand Your words in Luke 19:13 (NASB) that say, "Do business until I come…" so my steps will be orderly and my path cleared ahead for what You have prepared for me.

Comforter's staff, provide spiritual food for the journey. There are days when the travel seems long, and I need Your sustenance. Give me the ability to lock gaze with Your eyes, filled with a rich outpouring of love, so it may overflow onto each person who crosses my path. I will ponder over this pathway set before me and the glory of Your good pleasure.

REFRESHMENT
FOR THE SOUL

"He refreshes my soul. He guides me along the right paths for his name's sake."

PSALM 23:3 NIV

Where do you go to get away and become refreshed with God? Are you looking to find the "right" path? Me too. I find a path to God's door as I nest my faith into His providence and design to guide me through.

To find the path requires spending intentional and dedicated time with Him—our Leader, the Lord of heaven and earth. Matching up what the soul wants with what the spirit needs takes a bit of leaning in, learning to listen, engage, and leverage the personal investment of resources which are already in hands and spend the time it takes to learn how to use them more effectively. My experience is that these actions will produce the essential markers of guidance for the next stretch of the journey.

Question: How much are you willing to invest in the process?

Action Prayer: Lord, I come before You as the King of Glory and ask for the redemption of time. Only You can bring this unexplainable joy and answer. The gift is You, as we bring the first fruits of the evening or day and lay them in humble stewardship before Your throne. How sweet the sound of thoughts, questions, emotions, and desires for the two of us to share with great abandon. Each hidden gem discovered amidst the ruins is yet another treasure.

Thank You for selecting me for Your track of confidence in the best place and plan for this season of my life. This is my delight to find my first inquiry with You as the best course of action set for my day. Strengthen within me a spirit to enter in and listen to Your voice. Direct me to be trustworthy and true to reflect my actions and responses with the knowledge that You are the covenant defender, so in all seasons, I stay the course of Your care.

There is an incredible gift of oneness that awaits my personal spirit as You unite me as Your child to know Your masterful touch upon my life. My identity and destiny are prepared by the One who will lift and carry me across this threshold. Even now, You have equipped me for the next steps in stride with You. It is precious being a co-heir in Your kingdom's purposes. Amen.

25

GRACE AND BALANCE

"He makes me lie down in green pastures, he leads me beside quiet waters."

PSALM 23:2 NIV

God's gracious balance comes when we step into a place of abiding. It is His pleasure to see us resting in repose in the field He has specially prepared for us.

Question: What field has God prepared for you?

Action Prayer: In simple stillness, Lord, You have readied a forever place created just for me to occupy, especially during times when nothingness or lack of duties envelop me, and I am so easily tempted to hurry along to "do something" instead of resting in You. These are no arbitrary moments but times selected by the shepherd King, handpicked for my design. With gentle leading, I welcome Your staff to come near. I commend my personal spirit to listen to Your voice as You are singing over me.

The sound of heaven is best heard in the hush of silence as the notes brood over my heart. In the announcement of this special time and place, may it pierce all eternity like a bridal chamber with its living carpet of time prepared by the Bridegroom Himself with the details fitly set in place of righteous alignment.

The unforced grace reveals a treasure of Your design imprinted deeply within me. This journey has brought me to yet another bend in the river, just at the right time, season, and situation for this much-needed rest. I am forever grateful to be here with You as angels watch over me and write upon the scroll of my heart.

I bow my head and drink deeply from the fountain of refreshment prepared by these still waters offered by this stream of peace. This setting is so unfamiliar, and even the waters must be stilled and undisturbed, so I can learn to stay and drink a while. In peaceful solace, I sense the blanket of renewed confidence given to me by You, my protector, who will illuminate all that concerns me. Amen.

26

LACKING NOTHING

"The Lord is my shepherd, I lack nothing."

PSALM 23:1 NIV

The universal stating this, our Lord is always looking to give one hundred percent of Himself to His children, whether it's to one child or for many of His children. Our heavenly Father is the owner of all things and extravagant with all He gives. His gifts always arrive in a timely fashion, every time, without fail. Have you, like me, found it difficult to receive or accept a lavish and opulent gift? Perhaps the uncertainty of accepting that present has a deeper meaning. Could it be that our lack of receptivity stems from an inherent misunderstanding of how receiving gifts of love from a generous source is really a part of our limited perspective of God?

During a recent personal retreat, I found myself in disbelief regarding a generous gift from a friend. She offered the use of her lovely home for an extended time. The accommodations and surroundings were fit for royalty, but I couldn't seem to settle down when I arrived there. At first, it was like sinking into the most welcoming of soft pillows while at the same time wondering when someone was going to come snatch my luxurious head support from underneath me.

Question: Has there been a gift you've had trouble receiving lately?

Action Prayer: Lord, untangle my mind and make me to want for nothing. Help me receive from this deep place of love and rest provided by Your care. I speak to my personal spirit to turn towards the beauty on display as You, my God, spend Your own currency on a habitation of peace. I will come, accept, and drink from this well of deep love now flowing from Your throne to me.

Open wide Your gates, oh my heart, as I choose to soak up God's unfailing ability to meet me in His abundant goodness. Lord, You secured the right settings, and my heart has longed for reconciliation of all things in this season. Father, gather me to Yourself and carry me into a place to receive with any occasion, relationship, and situation.

Bless me to lean into Your strong, steady arms and nurturing of my heart. I tune my ear to listen for the repeated patterns of movement and sound of Your heartbeat for me in this place. I choose to unwrap the gift of my King's presence with me, and it is good. I feel blessed because I am. May all manner of frivolous ways melt away into pools of liquid love as You, my Shepherd, pour out over me. Cause me to step in line with Your timing and order of this love flowing in as I receive the keys to unlock every part of my story. Amen.

27

SHINING A LIGHT FOR ANOTHER

"...He will answer him from His holy heaven with the saving strength of His right hand."

PSALM 20:6 NAS

The morning rain comes down, and my mind is filled with wonder and questions about what today will bring. As the day unfolds, subtle anger begins to stir inside me. My mood is mixed with resignation as I accept today probably won't be my own but that of someone else's plans and ideas. There goes my autonomy. People living with dementia are often so unpredictable. It stands to reason that their companion(s), such as myself, might have to build a bit of flexibility into the schedule to help accommodate the well-being of all those involved. So I find myself contemplating if it's going to be one of those rare days when a solemn peace lays over the daily tasks to ensure all is well, or will those hopes be dashed and hearts cry out, "Lord, how long must we endure these conditions?" Then more questions arise, "Is this really Your plan, God? Are You hearing our cries for healing?"

These are the everyday questions of one living with and caring for another whose journey has turned in a most unforeseen way. Dementia alters a person's physical, mental, and emotional responses away from soul level realities and sometimes becomes difficult to see their God-given design. The effect for the companion to consider is how, in caring for this excellent person living with dementia, might there come an opportunity to reflect more light about who they are.

By blood or choice, perhaps you're the one voicing aggravation with statements such as, "You don't know what it's like to live with them." And to that, I say, "No, I do not." There is no pain like that of a daughter, wife, husband, grandchild, sister, or brother who so wants to connect with their beloved as before but finds it near impossible to do so with their loss standing there right before their eyes. Now, as a caregiver watching over our charge, we witness a dimming recall of things present, past, or future to no avail.

Question: Has your loved one "left" but somehow remains?

Action Prayer: Lord, help me to hear with Your heart of love. You, Lord, do not forget what is being endured. I crack my heart open a little more for Your light to fill me with the heavenly sound of peace, preservation, and purpose for this day given to me to walk.

I choose to yield my thoughts and perception to Yours and this earthly assignment with my loved one until their last breath. Their days are numbered by You, Father. Give me eyes to love and see, rest and build a place of welcome for Your presence, spiritual grit, and tenacity for the uncharted waters ahead.

Above all, I forgive, release, believe in my loved one, and pray on their behalf because I know You to be a God of unshakable ability to use all situations to teach us more when willing to learn. What has been chosen can change, and change is our only constant. How each one of us comes to yield to these ebbs and flows is sometimes such a mystery. Lead us back to Your words to come as a little child (Matthew 18:3 NKJV), especially when the way seems unclear.

We are each shrouded in a cloak of fragile humanity, and with Your acceptance and infusion of stamina, we can carry on for the next steps ahead. Thank you for the saving power always laid before us as Your gift. May it not be lain in the dust another moment. I choose You and am grateful for trusting me with this precious soul to love well as part of Your life's lesson plan for me.

God, You have made room for my life to add what really matters, so much more than I had imagined. Release Your light in me to know and value the good and perfect gift sent to me in fallible humanity. Help me to set my expectations on You, Your invitation, and unfailing love ready to save. Amen.

28

THE MESSENGER

"Better a poor but wise youth than an old but foolish king who no longer knows how to heed a warning."

ECCLESIASTES 4:13 NIV

The start of another day and the question arises in my heart, "Where will we go to find the answers?" The times and situations surrounding us now are eons beyond our comprehension to resolve. And this, despite living in the twenty-first century's Information Age, go figure. However, God points out that the possibilities in finding real truths may very well come from those we might least expect—the modest, often overlooked, and of a small social capacity like "a poor but wise youth" as described in the verse. Can we stop long enough to hear, listen, and accept the information at face value from someone so unknown, with no proven credibility, who is bringing us the truthfulness of a word?

These are the days to reflect as never before. It's scary to think the #MeToo movement could have materialized like the one first founded on the basis of an alleged sexual assault by a U.S. Supreme Court Judge.[3] Followed closely behind that case, further allegations and whistleblowing of a Hollywood A-lister on charges of criminal sexual assaults and harassment. And so the list of complaints against some of the world's most powerful people having committed a wide range of serious improprieties and injustices grows as the world continues to expose scores of those in high profile positions having become incapable of a common pause and reconsideration of their actions.

There are strike force teams deployed around the world to help address current unrest, wars, and medical conditions. While some call this the last days, a curse, judgment, or the result of sloppy haphazard living without a thought to consequence, I believe it's a combination of all these things. Today's dissemination of information has never been so rapid. We're able to witness enough atrocities and tribulations to knock the earth off its' axis live on our computers and broadcast sources. How are we supposed to respond? Should we solicit a mystic to find answers or just go hide? Again, it comes down to how each of us chooses to react, in the end.

Question: Is there someone in your life who has been trying to share a warning of some kind?

Action Prayer: Father, I invite Your light to give my spirit the ability to pause, breathe deeply, and listen to those who surround me. Help me hear, listen, and respond to the cries of the messenger longing to be heard. Give me the ears of Your heart, Lord, and to hold fast against the temptation to discount harshly spoken content due to the form in which it may come.

Bless me with Your solemn rest, heavenly Father, to submit the chatter to my human spirit who is connected to Your discerning work. If there is a best "next steps" through this perilous season, I surrender to hearing it from You. Give me ears to hear, listen, and rest as I lean in to hear from a heart of divine wisdom through these humble messengers. I choose to turn heaven-bound again and again with the strength of heart to recall and rest in Your omnipotent love toward me and all mankind. Amen.

29

THE DIVINE
NATURE OF LIGHT

"Through these he has given us his very great and precious promises, so that through
them you may participate in the divine nature, having escaped the corruption in the
world caused by evil desires."

II PETER 1:4 NIV

Are you finding yourself in repeated patterns of fear? If so, ask
yourself this question, "Where am I sourcing my strength in
this situation, relationship, or circumstance to alleviate parts
of the pain of these emotions?" If you're feeling continuously
exhausted in your efforts to keep your fearfulness at bay, there's
every possibility the way you're going about it isn't working.
How we try and swat fear out of the picture might be doing
more harm than good and sucking our life energy dry. By nature,

we're meant to be problem solvers and figure things out, though, certainly not at the expense of our well-being. Just as we're not meant to solely rely on our foundations as exclusive means to gain strength and hope—that spot is reserved for God alone.

Our heavenly Father has a place of rest for His children, far removed from the need for any self-generated performance. Have you received some promises and words from God that have yet to eventuate? It might be time to dream again and review those promised gifts to see if there's anything you may have missed or have been unwilling to see. Welcome His light into a place of quiet contemplation and reflection so you might hear His voice more clearly and walk in peace beyond your understanding.

It is in the morning light, in the breaking of dawn over a new day, where fears are dispelled, and new scenes of promise begin to take form. Look into the birth of His light, breaking over those old familiar places and patterns within and allow fresh images of revelation to appear.

Question: Where is the source of your strength drawn from for a new life discovery?

Action Prayer: Jesus, I will look to You and ask for eyes to see what Your beautiful light exposes inside those unseen facets of my substance. "What is it, Lord?" I ask, then turn to examine and ponder the gifts stored in the hidden places of my heart. Give my eyes a new vision to see its substance, promise, and wonder of wonders. Your light will divinely kiss the gift and bring fresh promise to life. My spiritual father, Kent Newman, a wise apostle, once said, "Grace gives it, waiting reveals it, and faith distributes it."

Lord, help me to walk this out. Amen.

30

ASK YOUR QUESTIONS

"Will the Lord cast off forever? And will He be favorable no more? Has His mercy ceased forever? Has His promise failed forevermore? Has God forgotten to be gracious? Has He in anger shut up His tender mercies?"

PSALM 77:7-9 NKJV

God is not afraid of our questions. Actually, He takes pleasure in our willingness to wonder and invite Him into the most desperate times and seasons of our lives. In those hidden places of uncertainty, the Lord of heaven and earth has a singular resolve to hear our cries as His children. When situations and relationships seem to be going in the opposite direction to our prayers and desires, His ear is ready to listen.

Question: Lord, how can I share my hidden places of uncertainty with You?

Action Prayer: Father, help me sense You are here. I don't know the answer, but You do. Please guide me and help untangle the knots. Come in this hour, Father, and do this with me. Even if I must walk right down the middle of this chaos, help me grow and know the lessons I'm supposed to learn.

Bring Your light to guide me, so I know You have not changed Your mind about me or my current condition. Equip me with the weapons of warfare so I can discover the secrets of the truth of my position as Your child and what I am not seeing right now. Amen.

THE DELIVERER

"I sought the Lord, and he answered me; he delivered me from all my fears."

PSALM 34:4 NIV

His position is clear, the King of the universe has overcome all things. Fear that may cover us like a cloak offers no defense nor any protection. There are places of the heart in all of us where God longs to bring the truth of His comfort. When we find ourselves unable to receive God's care and nurturing or that of another's support, it might be a sign that our approach needs a little tweaking. The issue may be that we're relying too heavily on our own devices instead of waiting to see what God comes up with. Glory be to the Father; He is more willing to hear than we are willing to pray.

The fear center of the brain is a real place. It's an effective kit and a fascinating one, too. So much so that we can become a tad obsessed trying to understand its complexities while we're in action. Guaranteed, the minute we set a watch over our own behavior is typically when we begin producing a condition of hypervigilance. We now have fallen into a trap, filled by and afraid of our own shadow(s).

Living in a state of continual or excessive worry is not only miserable but will wear you down. We build a fort of self-preservation and protection that adds fuel to the fear bond.

Instead, focus on the invitation of God and His life-giving light that creates a space to receive. Investing in time with Him allows our hearts a new place to welcome deliverance.

Question: Where do you need a deliverer today?

Action Prayer: Lord Jesus Christ, in this situation (or) relationship, I need a deliverer. I ask for forgiveness for turning towards a mode of self-protection on my own to try and stay safe. The truth is I need the light that only You can give me in this circumstance. May Your justice and power bring the righteous and necessary rescue. My eyes are set on You, and I welcome You to sweep out the clutter and chaos of the enemy. Adjust my vision to see Your answers. Amen.

A GOD SET-UP

"I will sing to the Lord, because He has dealt bountifully with me."

PSALM 13:6 NKJV

What if God told you the cause of your current conditions were His doing, not the devil or anyone else, but Him? Could you rejoice as it says in today's verse?

Most of us struggle to find a place of recognition or acceptance when facing a distasteful situation. For example, your boss moves ahead with a plan, and you're not included. Maybe a friend down the street is starting to shy away from you for no known reason. Perhaps the brand-new car you bought needs major repairs. These are everyday events that, most of the time, will go unchecked as to whether you're getting set up by God.

A God set-up can be a pleasant surprise or a difficult occurrence to happen for a good reason out of the blue. Primarily, it's an arrangement by God to benefit or serve the person or sometimes a number of people in receipt. Keeping this in mind, what if that friend down the street is someone you've been praying for? Is there a possibility the sudden change in her demeaner is the result of God conditioning her heart to see or hear something? Given the same circumstances, would you be willing to listen to someone like the neighbor friend if they were to share a painful story with you or perhaps tell you about how they are feeling?

Recently, my new-to-me used car needed tires. So I took it to a tire store and had all four replaced. Part of the way through, the technician indicated one of my struts was weak and could break during the replacement process. I said fine and proceeded to get the new tires. That was it, or so I thought. My next stop was my car dealership to have a recalled part replaced. After the part was replaced, the mechanic came out to ask if I was aware one of my tire's struts was broken, and I was also missing several lug nuts (a very unsafe condition).

I was astonished. I thought the tire store would have repaired whatever had gone wrong when replacing the tires or at least let me know to go somewhere for further repairs. I was angry and returned to the tire store to ask what had gone wrong and what their plan was to replace my missing lug nuts. The assistant manager handled my complaint with finesse. He agreed it was a mistake to have let me leave without saying anything about the need for further repairs.

After a while, we wound up having a truly delightful conversation, and I was pleasantly surprised by the assistant manager's help when I let him know the situation. He promptly pulled out his personal phone and said he would connect me to his own preferred mechanic shop, and he did while I stood there. Admittedly, this was around the time I began to realize this was a God set-up. I had just spent the last eight months looking for a local, honest mechanic shop to take my car to for regular maintenance. Despite visiting several shops, I had not been able to find even one to measure up to my previous mechanics. I wanted someone with passion who cared about automotive matters and their customers—start to finish.

So over to the shop I went to meet "Bacon," a 28-year-old mechanic with enough certificates to fill a back wall. Having recently made manager, Bacon described the repair process, timeline, and even threw in a reduced price for the repair. With great enthusiasm, he shared how much he wanted my business and how he could fix just about any car around. I stood there amazed. I had found my new mechanic through a divine set-up by the King!

I could have missed it by jumping through all those various hoops that didn't fit neatly into my plans for getting new tires. Yet, there was a plan and bountiful gifts from God. I let Bacon know how I sensed this shop was going to be my new "go-to" place for future car service. I brought the car in for repairs the following day with a new realization of just how large the God set-up had become. The crowning touch was to be told their services on my car for the day were free! No charge for me and a new customer for them.

Question: Are you willing to invite the light of God into a complex situation?

Action Prayer: Bless You, Lord! I will rejoice, for You have my best interest in mind all the time. When distresses come my way, I can choose to look at how the bountiful way of Your handiwork can be found right in the middle of it all. Give me the eyes to see and a heart to receive. Amen.

33

HE SEES YOU

"If the foundations are destroyed, what can the righteous do? The Lord is in His holy temple, The Lord's throne is in heaven; His eyes behold, His eyelids test the sons of men."

PSALM 11:3-4 NKJV

Have we really come to understand the true immensity of our God? His is the final word of utmost supremacy as the ultimate judge over heaven and earth. In times of struggle and uncertainty, how do we trust our next steps will sustain traction for a safe and steady foothold to walk in His light? Our journey is often fragile. How we respond to the conditions along the way also reveals what areas in our hearts we've yet to secure. Wherever the grounds we walk lack stability is a place our heart is not yet at rest. Wandering through life in unrest is easy if you don't care; the hard part comes when you do.

With epic injustices destroying the nation's foundations by those who fall from grace, what then are the good people to do? Holy discontent should be where we begin with prayer to the only One who can build a sure foundation upon which our feet can stand. Hold strong and resist running away. Return to the place of conflict so your eyes might see the King as He comes. His reward is with Him. Even when our own eyes are closed, He sees what is happening and will not allow it to pass without being addressed.

Question: Is your footing secure or shifting?

Action Prayer: Our Savior, King, and one who is over everything from Your heavenly courts, hear my cry for justice. May my plea not be dismissed as invalid. Thank You for Your vindication to hear and review each detail and witness of the truth. A heavenly hearing will be held, and a verdict will be read.

There is not one who is exempt from Your eye. Your supreme laser vision sees from the beginning to the end. You, our advocate, are there and know our need for a deliverer. Even the sparrow, when it falls to the ground, is known by You. How much more You care for us in this test of our journey. We welcome the Chief Cornerstone, who is our solid foundation, not a shifting sand. Amen.

NO NEED FOR A LAMP

"There will be no more night. They will not need the light of a lamp or the light of the sun, for the Lord God will give them light. And they will reign forever and ever."

REVELATION 22:5 NIV

This verse once gave me much cause for pause and reflection, taking me back to a place and time in the late eighties with my son, Adam. It was an odd thing, yet it was as if I heard to not to spend any time planning about where we were to stay on our upcoming trip. This scripture echoed in my ear, "There's no more night" and I knew it to mean, His plan would be there to guide and direct in this next turn in the journey.

It's so hard to release my son to this foreign boys' school in upper New York state, but every need has been met—the scholarship for tuition, plane fare, rental car, and time away from work. *But*

*I'm not to make any arrangements for a hotel? This isn't easy Lord;
are You sure?* I was reminded to continue to step out and believe
that this plan would require the light of God to show the way.
My heart was busy breaking over the situation of releasing my
son to a place well over a thousand miles away. Knowing inside
that i was necessary and the right thing to do, but no less a
rough road to hoe. Each step had been directed, every one of
them, and so here I went —letting go, yet again to take hold of
a new and different way.

The plane landed and we set off in the rental car. My son
Adam asking, "Where are we going to stay tonight, Mom?" My
answer felt something akin to what Abraham must have said,
as he walked to Mount Moriah with his son Isaac to give as a
sacrifice. "The Lord knows," I said, and we continued in silence
without knowledge or sight. How hard it is to lean not on our
own understanding, and embrace the desperate sense of needing
His light.

We traveled first to see the school where an admission
appointment was scheduled for the following day. This school
was nestled along the edge of a quaint little town with rolling
hills and the sweet fragrance of fall which mingled in the air. A
year-round curriculum was offered to those who attended the
school of Freedom Village. As we sat there gazing at the school,
I inquired, "Okay, Lord, where to?" and heard a whisper in my
heart, "Go - one town back."

So one town back we went to find a single store that served as a post office, grocery store, and pool hall. I entered and asked the shopkeeper about hotels in the area.

He shrugged and remarked, "Only have one, ma'am. It's an inn at the bottom of the hill by the lake."

He indicated the innkeepers ran a bed and breakfast out of their home. He gave us directions, and we set out down the hill. Arriving along the banks of the lake, to find a large, rambling plantation home with the owner out in the yard raking leaves. I explain we were looking for accommodations for several days, and he cocks his head in thought. "I'm usually full up, but I've had several cancelations and have no guests staying at the moment. I would be glad to show you around, and you can have your pick from any of the rooms."

Wow! Adam and I looked at one another in amazement, and we ventured in to find four beautifully decorated bedrooms. We settled in and were welcomed by the mistress of the home, who quickly shared where we could find some supper and a restful place to lounge in their backyard. Out the door and two-story high, we were greeted by a waterfall cascading down majestic rock formations into a pool below which led to the nearby lake.

Isn't it amazing how things can turn out when we choose to release ourselves to follow God's lead?

Question: Is there an area in your life where God is asking you to let go in a new and different way?

Action Prayer: Lord, on Your cross, I put to death my need to be needed and to control or manipulate. I ask for Your wisdom because it is so extremely diverse. You have a huge number of ways to bring truth and wisdom to me. Forgive me for the limited ways in which I have believed You could resolve the condition I have found myself in. I repent for my reaction to over-control or under-control and now see how my continual attempts to control have put me in the position of judge or victim. I recognize and renounce these roles.

I choose, by proclamation, to receive the grace You have extended to me and release anything (person, place, condition, land, time, etc.) to You to accomplish the necessary work. I submit all that I am and all that I have back to You and welcome Your illuminating light to dispel the darkness within me and dismantle the strongholds of flesh and fear. I invite my God-given authority to come and reveal the many-colored sides of love prepared specifically by You in all manners of being.

Help my heart to trust and be free to live, laugh, run, and risk. I ask for You to restore and redeem every place in my spirit where I have been torn apart. Restore the fragments of my soul and spirit and give me the inner strength and resilience with human relationships to see others as they are truly meant to be. I need Your vision of grace, love, and wisdom along this journey. Amen.

35

A HIDING PLACE

"The Lord also will be a refuge for the oppressed, a refuge in times of trouble."

PSALM 9:9 NKJV

There will always be times of trouble in civilization. And historically, when all human attempts to thwart the social ills of society fail, it's no wonder some might consider the possibility that what's been set before us will never change. The principles of the universal law of change are obvious, nothing stays the same.

The law of change is the lesser known of the universal laws to exist. It is known that the universe is always changing or able to change. Everything is pretty much in a constant state of flux—to find balance despite what man might hope or desire. Man-made laws of ethics, or lack thereof, in communal living and the governance of society are an interpretation. Universal laws are absolute principles, and although change may not occur immediately, it does inevitability.

Either way, the point is God is not controlled by time. The fruition of His contributions will appear at His chosen moment and right on time. Evolution will happen because change is the only certain thing in this world.

The issue is this, where do we take cover during times of change? When we try and solve issues using logic, there can be an overload to the potential routes to avoid in order to minimize the impact of an on-coming transition. Many take shelter in their abilities, businesses, money, time, energy or other modalities in an attempt to divert trouble.

There is a place of breakthrough inside the refuge of the light of Jesus as we invite Him into the pivotal moment of change. He comes with masterful elegance, moving across time and space to bring every element into perfect position for the exquisite work to accomplish His plan.

Question: Where are you finding refuge in these days of trouble?

Action Prayer: Lord, I choose to respond like the psalmist describes, as one who has been oppressed and in need of refuge—in You. When I find myself in the middle of a cruel injustice, restrictive posture, or some burdensome issues coming my way with undaunting regularity, help me to choose to look to You and invite Your light to shine like the morning sun amidst the change which has brought me trouble and strife.

Cause my heart to know, even when the trauma seems relentless, to see Your light dispel the darkness. I rest on a sure foundation designed by You to become my footbridge to freedom under Your wings of protection. Give me the strength and will to move with the change You are pointing out. The essence of my purpose begins and ends at Your feet. I choose to cast my pride and vanity down, Lord Jesus, You are my true and perfect refuge. Amen.

36

HE REMEMBERS

"When He maketh inquisition for blood, He remembereth them:
He forgetteth not the cry of the humble."

PSALM 9:12 KJV

"Language-ing the indescribable" is a phrase I've heard to describe the pain brought on by trauma. One of the milestones on the pathway to the other side of trauma is to find your own words for what has happened. This practice, in my opinion, although not conventional, has proven successful in personal breakthroughs because God does not waste any pain. He wants to hear your voice and welcomes your expressions to be heard before Him in the courts of Heaven. When the verdict is reached, His light pierces through the darkness and the pain of the trauma. God Himself "nails it" with voracious certainty to the cross and pronounces it dead.

The unfolding of your story and the ability to tell it is part of what God uses to breathe life into your human spirit, soul, body, and heart. He longs to hear you and light your way back to life.

Question: Do you need a new language to express the trauma you have experienced?

Action Prayer: God, You are not caught unaware and will not let this slip by from Your sight. God of heaven and earth, remember and vindicate me. There is no doubt You have Your finger on the very core of the issue. There is no forgetting in Your vocabulary regarding the cries, shrieks, tears, fears, waves of shock, pain, and groans heard in my voice.

Lord God Almighty, I choose to believe You are on it, though hidden from my view at this very moment by the shadows of foreboding. I welcome the piercing light that reveals the many facets of love and warfare on my behalf. Let me hear Your righteous, long overdue word for a better season of good fruit. We cry out, "Come, oh Lord, come." Amen.

37

WHERE IS HOPE?

"Oh! May the God of green hope fill you up with joy, fill you up with peace, so that your believing lives, filled with the life-giving energy of the Holy Spirit, will brim over with hope!"

ROMANS 15:13 TM

Hope can be contagious, even as you walk down the grocery aisle and strike up a conversation with a total stranger. In my experience, this type of chance meeting can spread a spirit of positivity, where fresh hope is imparted, like a fresh spirt of new growth on a tender plant. We're fortunate when this turns out to be the case, as not all chance meetings are created equal. Some wind up hopeless and may even be dismissed as irrelevant and brushed away like unwanted crumbs.

I came across a gentleman in the store the other day, and he was talking to himself as he scanned the canned goods section. I stopped and asked how the conversation was going. He immediately provided me with an analysis of the products set before him and how unlike they were to those in his former country of origin. He then continued to chat about other sundry topics.

At no point did he make any requirement, demand, or request for me to engage in dialog, so I just stood there in connected interest, adding my two cents here and there. The ebb and flow of our discussion was unforced and became fairly rhythmic as we carried on. It somehow felt as if I had known the fella for a lot longer—-having struck up such an easy rapport. There we both were, fully engaged in the canned foods aisle, conversing in what seemed like the eternity dance of some good ol' meaningful humanitarian discussion. It left me filled with joy all day, as I'm pretty sure it did also for him, as well.

When we intentionally take time to relate to another and hear more of their story, it builds blocks of hope and courage into the structure that build community. Though this bridge might be a bit rickety at first, each board of connection eventually becomes stronger as it's nailed together with trust, faith, and the life-giving energy of the Holy Spirit. It's these materials that offer the possibility of more life and added blessings.

We're all given opportunities to bless one another, even in the small, day-to-day, routine moments. None of us can know the gems of joy we might pass along which bring someone into a new place of transformation. Sometimes, our presence can unlock an ordinary interaction and shape a whole new form of nurture to burst open even the most dammed up of hearts. Bring your hope to the light. It counts!

Question: Where can you share some hope today?

Action Prayer: Lord, I want to share Your hope with humanity. I want to overflow. Thank You for showing me it can be done in the everyday arena of life. Please send opportunities my way, and give me the ability to spot them when they come. I invite Your light! Amen.

38

ALL THINGS HOLD TOGETHER

"The Son is the image of the invisible God, the firstborn over all creation. For in him all things were created: things in heaven and on earth, visible and invisible, whether thrones or powers or rulers or authorities; all things have been created through him and for him. He is before all things, and in him all things hold together."

COLOSSIANS 1:15-17 NIV

There is nothing so intricate as how a cellular structure is formed and then functions. There, amid nothingness, creation bursts forth with new birth and multiplication. A fancy term called cellular respiration is where elements are received by the cell and produce an extravagant display of energy.

No single element alone can produce the product. It is only when the elements meet with one another and meld together does this phenomenon of energy occur. Through this combination, momentum is produced, and two new elements are created that go on to accomplish other new functions of life.

The wonder of life is imprinted into the Creator of heaven and earth. Even the very cells of our body are fashioned to welcome the light of His transforming power.

Question: Is there a place in your life where you long to be held together more solidly?

Action Prayer: Lord, I ask a rhetorical question, where can we go from Your Spirit? Life is all around. New birth is happening all the time and is ours for the taking. I am discovering that I must choose it first. Sometimes, I feel like there is nothing left for me to give, but then I remember I can come and bring myself to You.

In this coming, I understand what is given is only made possible by what I've first received. The extraordinary miracle happens when I bring my humanity to You, Father. Hold me together,

Lord Jesus, and combine my spirit with Yours for that sparkle of life-changing power to move forward. The result of our intimate union is the element to produce a God-given supernatural energy needed to build out a heavenly foundation within me. Thank you for holding me together in the process. Amen.

39

CONNECTIONS

"For it pleased the Father that in Him all the fullness should dwell, and by Him
to reconcile all things to Himself, by Him, whether things on earth or things in
heaven, having made peace through the blood of His cross."

COLOSSIANS 1:19-20 NKJV

To experience a certain sense of realization and awakening at
the end (or near the tail end) of a difficult event is our natural,
God-given path and a gift to moving forward. Thanks to God's
incredible healing process we can have an impact and favor.
There is a source or heartbeat all its own to trauma. This is when
at last we'll see more clearly what happens after an event and the
mark it's left behind and within. Trauma imprints a pathway not
just in one area alone but can seep into the body, soul, heart, and
even the spirit. This experience might occur after a car crash, for
example, when we find ourselves reluctant to drive again and

overly fearful when taking the wheel. This is because the residue of the traumatic event has built bonds that affect our brain and emotions (the latter, which is part of our soul). Repeated trauma occurring over time continues to leave inroads in our lives that continue to show up and affect our choices, beliefs, and values.

Knowing how trauma works can lead to new depths of understanding about the importance of welcoming the light of Christ into every area of our lives. Connecting our journey with His allows for a revelation; perhaps, it's something you have been dreaming of or desired but has seemed beyond your reach. Linking your story with His is the key.

When you bring your part of the story and tie it to the work of the cross, which Christ has accomplished, the rest of the story comes to light. Jesus Christ's sacrifice is enough and continues to bring the light to our condition to reveal, restore, reconcile, and bring righteous restitution.

This union, as the verse tells us, spreads a blanket of relationships in remarkable and unprecedented ways that have not been seen or experienced before. Requesting God to bring His perspective to our current circumstance leads to new ways, internally and externally, to discover untapped assets and resources. Developing this strategy comes by keeping an open invitation through our personal spirit during and following difficulty as an avenue for our heavenly Father to show us more about what, why, and how to bring value from what seems beyond saving.

Question: Are you struggling with a difficult period or event? Consider asking your heavenly Father to show you what He wants to impart to you through this circumstance.

Action Prayer: Lord, I come and choose to link my personal spirit, soul, heart, and body to Your way and plan. I need Your viewpoint on what You desire to reveal as a masterpiece in disguise. My ear is tuned for the sound of Your heartbeat, and I look for You to bring a spectacular union, strength, authority, and life into this situation. I welcome You to enlarge my heart to receive the fullness of this reconciliation of all things. Amen.

40

REDEEMABLE

"Those from among you shall build the old waste places; You shall raise up the foundations of many generations; and you shall be called the Repairer of the Breach, The Restorer of Streets to Dwell In."

ISAIAH 58:12 NKJV

A place of safety is available right in the middle of what may seem the most uncertain circumstances. In these most perilous of times, it's in our best interest to answer with an affirmative response. God is shouting out His plans today on the earth. The time is upon us to hear the loud and clear invitation being sent for us to join Him. So listen closely and tune the heartstrings of your heart to the music of the maestro's hand as you are His finest instrument.

Although the musical notes may sound a little off key at present, remember, your story is not yet complete. The sounding of the trumpet will soon become clear, stronger, and in perfect pitch as you seek to harmonize with a heavenly flow in beat with Kingdom realities that serve a vital role to fulfill and redeem everything.

God is asking us to bring all the hidden tragedies, traps, and seeming wasted years to His living water for cleansing and take a look for newness of life to rise up. Each one of those traumas have a transforming power to become a resounding testimony on the earth. Those supposed "waste places" are the missing pieces for many and life lessons for yourself and others.

Bring all the broken pieces so a kindled heart of love and passion can set in order the fragments for repair. Broken places, promises, or betrayals? Lift them up to His light for His holy fire purges and purifies. The flames of God's presence will burn away the impurity, the waste will fall away, and a hidden treasure buried so very long ago will be revealed. The gems of your story hold a precious song waiting to be sung. Be one aglow with His light and breakthrough to the call and sight of the gleam and glory of restoration that has been prepared just for you.

Question: Will you have an affirmative response to heaven's call today?

Action Prayer: Lord, how precious is the ointment of Your redeeming love, flowing down from Your throne and covering my deep cracks of brokenness. Gaze now on the foundation sealed by Your blood, restore and ransom the breaches within me for all eternity. I hear Your call to me and respond as one ready to be a light-bearer reflecting the undying flame of Your glory.

You have been calling me to build, take dominion, overcome, and embrace all at the same time. No one can do this without You. I pray for courage and strength as I embark on the journey of restoration by looking into the wounded place where trauma has ravaged. Because the Word says You will "restore the streets to dwell in," I ask for ointment for my eyes to see the gift of my own story gleaming amongst the rubble. Amen.

41

SONG OF LIGHT

"But he who received seed on the good ground is he who hears the word and understands it, who indeed bears fruit and produces: some a hundredfold, some sixty, some thirty."

MATTHEW 13:23 NKJV

Blurred or blessed, the people arrive. Some sure of a breakthrough, others stranded amidst the great unknown that looms beyond the dew-drenched morning. All is a mystery as each one is beckoned to rise and bring forward their part. How truly divine are the impressions of a collective humanity chosen to be part of an already perfect story.

Slowly, the stage is revealed as the curtain is raised. Another new day births, an opportunity to present ourselves on display as lilies in His garden. In states of nyctinasty, the flowers, tucked in at night, loom large to unfurl a masterpiece and symmetry of life. Implementing such a grand effort takes the courage of a lion. And with His plan unveiled, a choir of song resounds, lifting freely into the coldness of the dark night, a melody of hope.

This world longs for such a song to be sung as it bemoans with refrains that shatter the sound of common sense and decency. The Lord hears each of our voices and is poised to resound within a framework of symphonic rhythm in harmony with His plan through creation. Our response in kind, with heaven's song resonating within, we reach a crescendo of music set across creation—TOGETHER. All things, yes, all things working together for good.

Question: Can you pause and let His light help to reveal your song?

Action Prayer: Lord, I choose to quiet myself and listen, opening my inner landscape to hear the sound pouring down and through me. I set this sacred time apart to receive the drops of heaven-sent sounds. May Your light reveal creation and set the order in simplicity, a ready place where a pure pitch brings breakthrough. Lord, I give You my story with all its broken state of wreckage to receive Your Holy Spirit to fill the cracks with refiner's gold. Bind it all together to produce a healing salve to bring forward good seed in the ground of my heart. Amen.

42

HIDDEN TRAITS

"But with me it is a very small thing that I should be judged by you or by a human court. In fact, I do not even judge myself. For I know of nothing against myself, yet I am not justified by this; but He who judges me is the Lord. Therefore, judge nothing before the time, until the Lord comes, who will both bring to light the hidden things of darkness and reveal the counsels of the hearts. Then each one's praise will come from God."

I CORINTHIANS 4:3-5 NKJV

Most often, waiting patiently is not one of our strongest character traits. For example, we might find ourselves in a line of traffic slowed along some road by an enormous truck up ahead and begin chomping at the bit. Or maybe we feel ourselves running short of patience with the shopper who won't get out of the way but instead takes up room meticulously rearranging their cart full of groceries for purchase at check-out. Grocery stores are classic places to try our patience. I'm slightly amused why, seeing as how it's the perfect place for it, we don't see massive food fights erupt. Everybody knows about that one check-out clerk notorious for leisurely scanning through the items like they've got all the time in the world.

What happens to us in those minutes of waiting to test our patience? Is it some sinister, hidden part of our true nature bubbling to the surface? In observing my own behavior, noticing when these traits crop up can come as quite a shock. So I am learning to consider them as realizations—a messenger of light bringing a fresh perspective to just how far I, too can stray from the core of my inner peace.

Question: Are there some hidden traits found in your responses that come as a surprise?

Action Prayer: Lord, You know how opposition casts a shadow across life. Heavenly Father, keep showing me what is on my own plate by way of my hidden responses. Reveal the hidden patterns through my day-to-day situations and relationships so all the dark areas within me can come to know Your light. I invite divine justice and judgement to bring clear knowledge of what is within me, at the heart of the matter. I confess, I need Your work of repentance and transforming power to change me. I long to be Your shiny one who carries the light of Jesus. Amen.

43

BREATH OF GOD

"Who redeems your life from destruction, who crowns you with lovingkindness and tender mercies, who satisfies your mouth with good things, so that your youth is renewed like the eagle's."

PSALM 103:4-5 NKJV

Is there a place in your life that once held your dreams but now you find has been cashed in for what is said to be "the real deal?" Perhaps that old dreamy path seems more like a road riddled with rot, filled with the very bare bones and potholes of your living conditions and circumstances beyond all logical understanding. Pretty sure we can all agree that waking up to your brain telling you, "Darlin, you've arrived, and this is all there is!" leaves us feeling flat.

There is a place of release, and your heavenly Father encourages us by saying, "Bring those dreams to Me."

God desires to take the fragile construct of our dreams and lovingly holds them close to His heart, breathing the breath of Himself into them once more. The outcome and verdict of our trials are sure to be seen through the lens of His relentless and fierce love towards us. New mercies and sparkles of light are readied from heaven for release into the cracks of those broken dreams, like gold from His treasure house.

Question: Are you moving towards fulfillment of your dreams?

Action Prayer: God, You are good, and a good Father you are. You placed those dreams within me long ago, and today, I ask You to breathe renewed life into them. Your plans and desires are to crown me with a life of activation and an ever-outstanding badge of honor. Though crumbs of fear and distress might fall from my lips, I welcome Your breath of life upon my dreams. Fill me with Your thoughts, vision, and work so that my strength and vision are renewed like an eagle. Amen.

INCHING ALONG

"Stand in awe, and sin not: commune with your own heart upon your bed, and be still."

PSALM 4:4 KJV

There are four distinct instructions in this tiny verse. To consider them, we might ask, "Where will we go as this world continues to steer off course? Does it matter? Does God really hear our prayers anymore, or are there special words needed to get the Lord's attention?"

These are just a few of the questions which may cross our mind when we find ourselves in the middle of an unwarranted or unwanted predicament, the kind that brings us to our knees and puts a screeching halt to any existing joy—not in terms of years gone by or those living in the past, but right now.

This verse of Psalms contains words that refer back to the power of God in the beginning where He commands over all things. He is the redeemer and an absolute truth; however, it's ours to choose whether or not to connect in relational life with Him. There is no place where God is not, so when you find yourself at the end your rope, super worried and lost. Look for His light, let go and seat yourself in His presence, follow His plan, and soak up the pleasure of being His beloved child. This is an infusion for our hearts so we can be more whole through a knowing of Him and His love for us.

Question: Which of the four areas of instruction in this verse seem highlighted for you?

Action Prayer: Lord, with a quiver of holy fear and humble heart, I come to bow at Your feet. There is so much I do not yet understand. Can You hold all these unknowns? Keep me so I do not turn away from You in times of uncertainty. Turn my face to see You and Your ways through times of difficulty.

Bathe me in Your rest. Have me recline in Your steadfast arms so my heart can grasp and settle into what You are teaching me. Heavenly Father, bring me to the end of myself and cause a stillness to look up and embrace Your ways, plans, and timing and know the joy of my salvation in Christ. Amen.

NOBLE SUBJECT ARISE

"O ye sons of men, how long will ye turn my glory into shame? How long will ye love vanity, and seek after leasing?"

PSALM 4:2 KJV

There are people around you who would rather see you fail than get back up and go at it again. So how will you respond? No doubt, within community there are just as many of those who do not favor any of your success or change as there are people who do. Does that surprise you?

The issue is not whether those around you are successful in making you out to be the bad guy. Fabricating a "tale of shame" regarding someone's reputation can be easily concocted within just a few short sentences or minutes for that matter. The real issue is will *you* believe what is said about you. For example, there in the corner lays a garment ready for donning. We'll call it, "the robe of shame"—woven from words of distain, fear, and lies. Will you get dressed up and wear it as your symbol of truth, your regalia of submissiveness?

The remainder of the verse concerns the source of the intent to destroy—as referring to King David. This verse applies to his own son, Absalom, who was indeed very intent to tarnish and conquer his father's crown and kingdom.

In the broil of accusation and rumor, we might decipher this verse in terms of an accusation to you who represents what "they" cannot obtain on their own merit. Many have tried to gain success and joy, only to find the space can be leased for but a short while and it holds no permanent place to abide. How can that be?

There are many people who will not have the courage it takes to become a noble subject of the King of kings, Christ Jesus. They would much rather rent a seat for a time until it no longer suits their comfort zone. The requirements for each one of us is the need for a direct connection with the true light source. Anything other than a straight and honest one-on-one relationship is merely a vain attempt at avoidance.

Question: Is there a deterrent of some kind, standing in the way of you joining with the truth you have not yet recognized?

Action Prayer: Lord, I am choosing to take a stand as Your noble subject. I understand now there will be times to walk against the winds of living an ordinary way of life. Teach me how to walk in the truth and excellence as Your gallant warrior. I embrace this assignment that has been birthed by Your Spirit and not by human means. May my position, assigned by You, the King of Glory, be immovable against all opposing forces. Open my eyes to every element of my birthright so nothing is lost. God, I believe You have my back, and I am leaning into this truth. Amen.

46

MERCY IN
THE MAKING

"Have mercy upon me, O Lord; for I am weak: O Lord, heal me; for my bones are vexed."

PSALM 6:2 KJV

The author of this psalm is keenly aware of the place of his need. Gazing into the invitation, he writes of a longing to be found in the essence of mercy. Could it be a request for the precious attribute of mercy to be slathered out like a bar of soap and all traces of the issues at hand to simply disappear? Or could it be more of a plea from one who knows what it means to be broken and desperate for reprieve.

Though nothing changed along the story of this psalm, it bears a mark of eternal hope. As a star glimmers in a black sky, the call for mercy gleams amidst the shattered pieces of a soul. Despite the heartache, mercy permeates the crushed fragments and light is found. These tiny slivers of light bring into focus a myriad of color, splashed across the frame of existence. The knots along the grid are unlocked and the birth of mercy arises from the incense of a prayer.

Letting mercy be your bedfellow is found through understanding the perplexities and the message they are speaking to you. In the verse, we see David knew from the weariness of his own body the memory of how our entire being can voice a cry for mercy if we will but listen.

Question: Where do you need mercy to meet with you today?

Action Prayer: Teach me, oh Lord, how to apply mercy like a salve to the places in my life where my bones are aggravated and seem so brittle and dry. I choose You above all. Demonstrate through my life how Your mercy and truth meet and are on display as Your reward. As it is in heaven, so may I sense Your strength and healing balm here. Amen.

47

HE PRESERVES

"I will lift up mine eyes unto the hills, from whence cometh my help. My help cometh from the Lord, which made heaven and earth. He will not suffer thy foot to be moved: he that keepeth thee will not slumber. Behold, he that keepeth Israel shall neither slumber nor sleep. The Lord is thy keeper: the Lord is thy shade upon thy right hand. The sun shall not smite thee by day, nor the moon by night. The Lord shall preserve thee from all evil: He shall preserve thy soul. The Lord shall preserve thy going out and thy coming in from this time forth, and even for evermore."

PSALM 121 KJV

Psalm chapter 121 is among a series of fifteen chapters in the Psalms known as "The Song of Ascents," including chapters 120-134. These songs were actually sung by those making pilgrimages to various annual festivals such as Passover in Jerusalem. Interpretations of Psalm 121 describe Jewish priests singing these Songs of Ascent and responders answering in kind as they hiked through the mountains along the incline to Jerusalem, as well as walking up the many steps to the city's temple. The Psalms singers sang the Songs of Ascent referring to the constellations along the way, the terrain, weather conditions, politics, heaven, and the Lord's assurances, to name a few. There was a deep and comprehensive recognition of the vastness both in heaven and on earth and what it meant to present before a Holy God.

The Online Etymology Dictionary defines ascend as follows: "move upward;" from Latin *ascendere* "to climb up, mount;" of planets, constellations, "come over the horizon;" figuratively "to rise, reach."[4]

While Psalm 121 is rich in meaning and wide-open to interpretation, for the sake of discussion, we'll consider these verses in terms of preserving our spirit, beliefs, determination, and God's infinite, transient love over all our states of being along life's journey.

To preserve something, several actions must take place. The outcome of the process depends a lot on the integrity of all the parts. Much like the techniques involved in a clinical trial or scientific experiment, a "controlled" or "constant variable" is required. With no exception, the constant we need is the very essence of God Himself. It is His existence that transcends time, space, and matter, a type of ground zero for whatever else is to be added. We are part of His design from before the beginning. God delights to preserve and expand His Spirit within us. Our perseverance often requires that we remain in an absolute state of stillness while the heavenly alignment unfolds, and there as we receive, His will preserves all that concerns us.

Question: How can this principle of preservation help you keep a steady gaze on the hills from whence comes our help?

Action Prayer: Lord, help me remain in position. I know You will come, and You are never late. Your timetable is not like mine. Lord, I release my timeline to Your cross in surrender. Cause my tenacious heart to drink deeply from a place of knowing You have not forgotten, and You care about the condition I am in. I choose to set my feet on the solid ground of Your keeping. I Corinthians 10:26 (NIV) says, "For, the earth is the Lord's, and everything in it." Your greatest joy is to maintain and keep that which concerns me without delay or decay. Amen.

THE RIGHT TOOL

"Which of you, if your son asks for bread, will give him a stone? Or if he asks for a fish, will give him a snake? If you, then, though you are evil, know how to give good gifts to your children, how much more will your Father in heaven give good gifts to those who ask him!"

MATTHEW 7:9-11 NIV

It's plain and hopefully common sense to have the right tool for a job. If I use my rubber tipped hammer to drive a nail, the hammer tip is inclined to become damaged. And it's very likely the nail won't go very far either. Evidence shows this fundamental concept to hold true—you really can't do the job if you don't have the proper devices for implementation.

This being the case, then why, at times, do I take little shortcuts in hopes to accomplish a task without the right tool? The answer is most likely because it might initially work, at least for a short period of time. When I receive a given result, my stunted patience cries out, "Ok, what's next?" A sense of accomplishment overtakes me and a desire to be done with it. Then with self-satisfaction, I'm usually on to the next thing.

Have you noticed that when it comes to a spiritual journey with God, there seems to be an extraordinary lack of wiggle room for taking a shortcut? Yes, things may work out for a while and even gain some traction, but that type of gain usually doesn't have much sustainability. A lack of progress begins to appear, and eventually, we discover the tool we used was not the best one for the job. We often take the long way around to find this out as well. So it stands to reason that the right tool fit for the right job must first be tested. If we're lucky, it might just dawn on us to rethink our approach, and before reaching for that handy tool for a project or idea, we should first ask.

Question: Do I have the right tool(s) needed in my current situation, and is this project for me to do or for God to do?

Action Prayer: Lord, bring Your light to help me see Your plan with the right tool, right fit, and purpose. I am Your servant and commit to research, investment, and application of Your key strategies until this treasure can be unlocked to the fullness of Your kingdom purposes. Thank You for Your Word to me which says, "God gives good gifts to His children." (Paraphrased, Matthew 7:11). Amen.

49

WEIGHT OR RELIEF

"Oh that my grief were thoroughly weighed, and my calamity laid in the balances together! For now it would be heavier than the sand of the sea: therefore my words are swallowed up."

JOB 6:2-3 KJV

Grief can feel like wearing a pair of heavy boots. They drag wherever we go. As Job points out, walking through a traumatic (calamity) event and expecting our emotional (grief) response to be of equal value and convenient would be nice, but it's not how we're built as human beings. If we were to attempt putting the trauma and pain into words at the exact time the trauma occurs, our words would just fall to the ground and turn to mush. This occurrence happens to all of us during the scathing torture that a traumatic event can bring.

Our brains are designed to track along a system of neural pathways, sending messages from one part of the brain to another. When faced with immediate danger or trauma, these nerve tracts literally close off in order to protect us from further harm. Our brain's reaction to trauma requires us to take a step back in order to allow our mental and emotional circuitry to catch up. This systematic way of coping is called "processing." But if we choose to mask the calamity and grief process with things like drugs, alcohol, business work, or denial, the trauma and grief become stuck and numbingly filed into a forgotten place. This is counterintuitive because this buried pain will remain somewhat dormant only to be released at a later time on an even larger scale when the next trauma event occurs.

The good news is that those heavy boots can be removed and the burden lightened. It often starts with plucking up the courage to come face to face with ourselves. Coming to terms with where "we are at" is a big recognition. Job had terrible things happen to him even though he was of honorable stature. He hadn't done anything untoward, yet some pretty bad things happened to him as the verse clearly states.

Finding relief from the weight of grief and the fear that can surround it can feel paralyzing and scary. Overcoming this fear requires action on our part. We must be willing to surrender to the reality of the trauma having happened and review some our choices that may have led us to this point. Embracing the hard work of the (re)processing that lays ahead softens the blow. God knows and cares about our grief and trauma. He knows how we are wired because we are made in His design. Breakthrough is possible because we are created for an extraordinary journey in partnership with Him!

Question: Can you recall a calamity or grief experience that needs revisiting with a different approach like those discussed here?

Action Prayer: Jesus, I invite You into this pain and grief and choose to embrace my part in it. Bring the light of Your Spirit and unlock the door of this prison. I cry out for *nasa* (which means in Hebrew: to lift up, to bear, carry, support, sustain, endure, to take, carry off or forgive) so Your light will bring liberty, freedom, and joy back into my life.[5]

I will respond to Your command, Lord, and not to the circumstances surrounding me. Give me wisdom not to be snared by worry or deceitful words. This place of trauma is not unknown to You, Father God. Help me to sense You here in this foreign land as I set You as a seal upon my heart to synchronize with Your righteous direction. Amen.

50

KEEPER OF THE HEART

"The Lord is thy keeper: the Lord is thy shade upon thy right hand."

PSALM 121:5 KJV

When reading this verse, I am reminded of some years ago when in the midst of a "valley of the shadow of death," I felt the need to know and feel the God who would be my keeper and protection.

In Hebrew, "keeper" is shamar (shaw-mar) meaning someone or something which hedges in; like a barrier, often with thorns.[6]

Making our way through a traumatic season in search of our "keeper" is often fraught with needle-sharp corners and jagged edges. In the place of deep trauma, it feels impossible to keep our grip, and we fail to hold on, no matter how admirable our intentions may be. It is at this point that our faithful Lord is vividly known as a safe place to land. God, "thy keeper," holds on to us, protects us, and keeps us as a Father should his precious child. The shade of His presence casts over my right hand, giving me strength, ability, and the impetus to carry on.

Question: How can I invite the Lord to come shine His light as my keeper today?

Action Prayer: Father, I openly share my heart and need for You. Come and be the keeper of all I am and can be. Keep me and direct me through the travail of this place. Strip every place where the enemy could have or has access to take me out or off-course from my God-given authority and design. I agree with Your Word; You make no errors. Show me the places in my heart that act as barriers to keep me from being all that I am meant to be. I invite Your light to shine. Bring me into this light of glory and peace. Amen.

51

THE ART OF WAITING

"Wait on the Lord; be of good courage, and He shall strengthen your heart; Wait, I say, on the Lord!"

PSALM 27:14 NKJV

Wait means "to stay where one is or delay action until a particular time or event."[7] By definition, to wait or waiting sounds relatively simple. In practical terms, the act of waiting is a little more complex and not humankind's greatest attribute. Paramount to its success involves remaining still, and that's something a lot of us least like to do.

As an example, it's a busy Friday afternoon and time to knock off work. You've put in a lot of overtime during the week and are ready to go home and wind down for the weekend. Then, bam! You've just been handed a last-minute "must do" project, and the deadline is in two hours. On top of that, a colleague needs briefing on it. Is your response to wait on God or furiously hurry along to get this last item off your plate?

Unfortunately, from my own experience, it's been more the latter, which left me slightly exhausted, resentful, and irritated for the interruption to my plans for a smooth exit into the weekend. On my drive home, I might typically begin the rehearsal with God about how unfair it was to have had to deal with that last-minute task that took forever to complete. Why didn't they come to me sooner? Couldn't it have waited until Monday? Don't they know I have a life too? They really don't know or care about me anyway. Knowing full well petulance does not become me, I might even wind up getting mad at being mad—an ultimate layer-cake of madness.

This type of scenario is a classic. So what if we were to apply the strategy described in this verse to "wait on the Lord?" Perhaps, we're relegated to a last-minute project, paper, or conversation, and instead of charging in, we find a quiet place to inquire in prayer. What is this, Lord? How am I to accomplish it in the given timeline? Is there an alternative way? Having practiced the art of waiting, I've discovered the best course of action is to refrain from making snap judgments and direct my questions toward Him instead. What is my part and when Lord? How freeing and simple the task becomes when we give it to God! Here are a couple of real-life examples from my experience.

Let's say a co-worker, we will call him Johnny, comes into my office asking, "Can you get your program bid out by this afternoon? The vendor needs it."

After asking several questions and seeing no other options, I agree. Practicing the waiting on God principle, I close my door and pray. I sense to call the vendor directly and review their request, so I do not leave anything out. The vendor shares a modified request and says, "The meeting they need it for isn't until Monday at 2:00 p.m." I schedule the work for myself on Monday morning's calendar and off for the weekend I went.

On another occasion, a colleague asked me to process a last-minute purchase of a large ticket item, so I prayed. Through the wisdom of God, I went back to that person and asked for their help to complete the order. Again, the work was done in record time, and the team approach led to a deeper mutual respect and appreciation.

Consistently, when applying God's principles in business, I have come away from the task refreshed not drained and joyous at the prospect of having worked in partnership with the King of the universe who delights in teaching me His ways.

Question: Could waiting on the Lord take on a whole new look for you considering these stories?

Action Prayers: Lord, thank You for the call to be more than a conqueror in You, especially in waiting. I am so grateful and welcome the light of Your presence into every step for my healing journey and in every area of my life. I pray also to be instrumental in helping others find more courage to trust that You are a redeemer of those who diligently seek You. Amen.

52

LORD, I'M LISTENING

"And the Lord appeared to him the same night and said, 'I am the God of your father Abraham; do not fear, for I am with you. I will bless you and multiply your descendants for My servant Abraham's sake.' So he built an altar there and called on the name of the Lord, and he pitched his tent there; and there Isaac's servants dug a well."

GENESIS 26:24-25 NKJV

When we brush past the daily moments of our life in a hurry, there can result a stockpile of missing pieces which are, in reality, crucial to the very essence of our humanity. Is it possible to slow down long enough to listen for God's direction and, like Isaac, stake your ground with intent?

The ability or inability to hear God has long been a universal quest since the creation of mankind. Our God-ordained desire to connect with a power greater than ourselves is innate within each and every one of us. When God spoke with Isaac, the words became a map and compass guiding the path. On another similar night, God provided instruction that strengthened Isaac for what was next and delivered deep revelation concerning the importance of his personhood.

Many of us long for an infusion of His light into our life's daily experiences to help us navigate more easily. It can be a mixture of anticipation or joy when stillness of uncertainty or in the midst of a uncertainty a breakthrough or timely sign comes. It's usually right on cue, custom designed, a special delivery without a whole lot of room for weariness and drudgery. Along with the act of hearing from the Holy Spirit is also the fresh current of air that lifts the personal spirit and can carry us toward a place of new possibilities and aspirations. Words spoken direct and clear, bring strength to an open-heart longing to receive news of value and birthright.

Question: Are you listening for what the heavenly Father has to say in your daily moments?

Action Prayer: Father, I take hold of Your Word and set camp to incline my ear to Your voice today. With thanks, I lay down my desires and heart longing to know and walk in Your beautiful footsteps. Give me heavenly nourishment from Your hand to help me build provisions for today and the days to come. I'm in awe that You delight in being known and heard by us in the middle of darkness. Come Father, Son, and Holy Spirit. Amen.

53

WAKE UP

"Get out of bed, Jerusalem! Wake up. Put your face in the sunlight. God's bright glory has risen for you. The whole earth is wrapped in darkness, all people sunk in deep darkness, but God rises on you, his sunrise glory breaks over you. Nations will come to your light, kings to your sunburst brightness. Look up! Look around..."

ISAIAH 60:1-4 TM

A shake-up is needed to open our eyes from relentless sleep. The arousal of a blazon announcement, the maiden of brilliance is here, the Holy Spirit blaring with an appeal for all of us to arise. The time of slumber is long past, and it is time to stir to the call within *you*.

Together we have seen a barrage of chaos aimed at us, seeking to shroud us with the grave clothes of despondency and despair. It's time to respond as God's "shining ones" out of an invitation that shatters the torrents, confusion, and questions and breaks open the unveiled radiance of colors God is waiting to reveal. A shake-up is needed to open our eyes from the stagnated compliancy that seeks to swallow up our very essence.

Question: Ask your personal spirit, where do I need to be awakened with more of God's light?

Action Prayer: God, I ask You to call my human spirit forward, to bring more clarity and insight to my spirit, and to strengthen my inner man (personal spirit), so I can connect more fully to the perspectives of heaven and not become sidetracked by the voices that tempt me to believe there is nothing left for me. I choose to receive the mantle of being a spirit, who has a soul and occupies a body here on the earth. Give me Your kingdom mindset and ability to rest in Your ownership of all things. Teach me to steward well—Your assignment within me. Amen.

ABOUT THE AUTHOR

Molly McNamara is the Founder and Executive Director of His Whole House Ministries. She is a licensed minister, author, international speaker, trauma practitioner, prayer counselor, and business coach. Molly's medical background combines the complexities of science and an individual's "God-given design" to reveal the corollaries based on biblical principles specific to a person's situation and pathways to healing and deliverance.

The mission of His Whole House, a non-profit organization, is to equip individuals and organizations to embrace their God-given design. Molly is a highly sought-after prayer minister and teacher specializing in trauma and toxic shame. Her vision is to serve the body of Christ throughout the world with transformational tools of "wholehearted living" as God's masterpiece.

The work was birthed out of Molly's own traumatic experiences and healing with many crossovers from science to spiritual wholeness while keeping with her passion and life work. At home, Molly finds sanctuary in her private study with her loyal Italian Greyhound, Jolie, by her side. In her quiet time, you can find Molly in her garden, swimming, traveling, writing, hiking with friends, and such.

www.hiswholehouse.org

ENDNOTES

1   "Extol." *Home: Oxford English Dictionary*, https://www.oed.com/.

2   "Manna." https://en.wikipedia.org › wiki › Manna

3   Gordon, Sherri. "What Is the Me Too Movement All About?" *Verywell Mind*, Verywell Mind, 24 Apr. 2022, https://www.verywellmind.com/what-is-the-metoo-movement-4774817.

4   "Ascend: Search Online Etymology Dictionary." *Etymology*, https://www.etymonline.com/search?q=ascend&utm_campaign=sd&utm_medium=serp&utm_source=ds_search.

5   *Strong's Hebrew*: 5375. אָשָׂנ (Nasa or Nasah) -- *to Lift, Carry, Take*, https://biblehub.com/hebrew/5375.htm.

6   *Strong's Hebrew: 8104.* רָמַשׁ *(Shamar) -- to Keep, Watch, Preserve*, https://biblehub.com/hebrew/8104.htm.

7   "Wait." *Home: Oxford English Dictionary*, https://www.oed.com/.

Made in the USA
Middletown, DE
04 April 2023